The First K-9 Trooper In

The New York State Police

James Keough

A collection of memoirs about my career
as a New York State Trooper.

Baretta and I

Dedication

I would like to dedicate this book to my wife, Blanche. She was always my biggest supporter and stood proudly by me. Blanche was a huge part of why I could do my job as well as I did. I knew she was behind me every step I took. I wish she could have seen her children as adults and see her amazing grandchildren.

****

Resemblance to any actual person by name, description or circumstance appearing in this book may be purely coincidental.

Table of Contents

4

Made in the USA
Columbia, SC
16 February 2021

(Second Edition)

Introduction

My name is Jim Keough. I entered the State Police on June 10, 1965. I wanted to become a Trooper since I was 12 years old. I enlisted in the Marine Corps when I was 18. I did a 4-year hitch, 2 years and 2 months in the Pacific and the rest was State Side. While I was in the Pacific I was a member of the Bravo Company 3rd recon and we worked mostly with submarines. My MOS was 0331, which was a machine gunner. I left my hearing somewhere in the Pacific. I also attended a diving school run by the US Navy at Pearl Harbor and graduated as a certified Scout Swimmer. After my tour with the Marines I was a Corporal. When the Marine Sergeant Major in charge of my unit interviewed me for reenlistment, I told him I was going to go to the NYSP to be a Trooper.

The State Police fed my family and kept me going to this day. I had four beautiful children and a wonderful wife. I also have seven grandchildren. My youngest son John is a Trooper who carries my badge, shield 2591.

The Academy

When I went through the academy, we had over one hundred in my class. I had some fine memories of the first few years on the job. We would study hard all week, be tested at the end of the week and if we failed they would tell us they were going to get rid of us. I remember being in a class on sex crimes and the instructor called on Recruit Robert Dunning and asked him, "If you were in your barn and put your penis in the mouth of a goat what would that be?" Dunning said "Great sir!" (The correct answer was having sex with an animal). Dunning had the entire class laughing very hard. Even the instructor thought it was funny.

Bob was shot to death at a domestic disturbance. The bad guy shot him at point blank range in the chest with a high powered rifle. Bob had a Sergeant with him who was also shot, but he killed the bad guy in the return fire. At the time of his death, Bob had served about twenty-two years. I was a friend of Bob Dunning and he used to bust my balls whenever he could. The last time I saw him, he was trying to get a picture of him holding a large beaver he had trapped with a funny caption beneath it in the Trooper magazine. The man was a born comic.

In that class there was also a man named Robert

Gaylo who was killed in a high speed chase with a stolen vehicle as a result of a traffic accident caused by the chase. They were good men, and great Troopers. They made the world a little better and safer while they were here.

My Mentor, Hank Youngblood

When I broke in on the job, my senior man was an Ex-Marine Named Hank Youngblood and he was hell on wheels. He was a great Trooper and he taught me everything he could in the time allotted to him. I think he felt sorry for me sleeping in the station, so one night he brought me home for dinner with his family. He had a very pretty wife and some beautiful children. One of his girls became a dispatcher in my zone and married my Zone Commander, Lieutenant Meyer. The only thing I could never understand about Hank is why he would want to work for Division Headquarters. He was a good Trooper and should have stayed on the road.

When I first got out of the academy, I was all concerned about what to do on the road. I was not sure what was expected of me and how I would do the job. Hank was my mentor and he did a good job keeping me on the straight and narrow. He showed me how things were done in the real world and he was a hard worker so it was easy to follow him. We worked in Monroe, New York in Orange County. At the time, it was called the

Monroe Station and it was in K troop.

One of the things that was unusual about this station is that there was an open case for the murder of a New York State Trooper. The case was still being investigated. I went through part of the case file and what I remember from it is that the Trooper was killed in southern Orange County on a road that went to Greenwood Lakes, New Jersey. He was found dead next to his motorcycle clutching a blue polka dot necktie. Bootleggers used the area that he was killed in before liquor was legal.

The other arrest Hank and I were involved with was with a group of teenagers who drove their car off the road and set it on fire. They were trying to collect on the insurance to replace the car. Hank was my partner that night and he ended up arresting all the people involved and bringing them to court.

The Monroe station had a division motorcycle assigned to it and Jim Quinn was one of the riders. Whenever I worked with Jim, I had a good time. When the motorcycles were being removed from the State Police Jim was upset and he kept calling me on the phone to see if anything new had occurred. He thought that I might have some news as I was assigned to the Loudonville Troop Headquarters. The entire inventory of State Police

Motorcycles were stored there before they were turned over to the State Park Police. Many Troopers were upset the cycles were turned over without painting them a different color. They just did not want to lose their ride.

When you were assigned to a station with a motorcycle, the senior was in charge of the motorcycle but all the men that were assigned to the machine and trained with it wanted to ride it. They would come to work an hour early to get a shot at it. If the assigned rider came to work and his motorcycle was gone, God help you! Some of the motorcycle men had their bullets chrome plated so they looked better when worn in the exposed type of loop carriers, which were not issue. Some of them had so much chrome on them they would not fit into the gun but they looked good. Most of the motorcycle men dressed well, looked good and worked hard so they were a plus for the job.

Obtaining a K9 Partner

When I arrived for duty one afternoon in 1975 to report for patrol at the New York State Police Loudonville Barracks, I received a call to contact Sergeant Walter Hornberger at the State Police Academy. I didn't realize then that the call I was about to make would change my life. I called him and he told me of an idea he had that involved the State Police obtaining working K-9's that would be trained to detect explosives. The Olympic Games would be training and competing in the future in New York and K9's would make things more secure. He wanted to know what I thought of the idea. At the time Sergeant Hornberger was in charge of the NYSP bomb squad. I was his main man for the "G" troop area of the State. I had previously gone to bomb schools for the State Police as well as when I served in the United States Marine Corps.

The Troop "G" patrol area covered 10 counties in and around the capital district. Sergeant Hornberger and I had searched quite a few suitcases and conducted bomb searches all over the state. I told him bomb detection dogs sounded like a good idea and I was excited about it. I had been reading articles about the use of dogs in explosive detection and they were all very positive. I knew this could change the way police work was conducted.

Two days later Sergeant Hornberger called me back and asked if I would be interested in obtaining a dog and training with it. I replied that it sounded good. At the time I didn't realize that I was going to be entering a completely new and better facet of police work with the dog as a companion. The next day the Sergeant advised me that I would be reporting to the Baltimore Police Department for K 9 training. There would be one other Trooper from the State Police joining me from Troop K located in Hawthorne, New York. I was designated the member in charge of the training detail.

Before I left for the training, a fellow State Police Loudonville Trooper, John Curry, initiated a conversation about the training detail I was assigned. I told him of my conversation with Sergeant Hornberger and that I was assigned to training with a K-9. To my surprise, the next morning I saw Curry in the Loudonville station and he advised me that he was on the detail with me and we would be going to Baltimore together. At the time I was surprised because he had no military or bomb handling experience and only 4 years on the road as a Trooper.

I had five years on the job when I went to the Redstone Arsenal in Huntsville, Alabama for bomb training and I worked on the New York State Police bomb detail prior to being asked to train as a K-9 handler. I had vast knowledge of bomb detection and I was certain I was highly qualified. Another Trooper named Art Krug also joined us for the training.

When we reported to Sergeant Jerry Darby at the State Police Academy for vehicle assignments, we were advised that only one vehicle was available. John Curry grabbed that set of keys and I was told they would attempt to locate another one for me. Soon after, a second vehicle was located and we were on our way. Shortly after arriving in Baltimore, we reported to a Sergeant from the Baltimore Police Department by the name of Tom Nott. Sergeant Nott was a very senior member of the Baltimore Police Department. We also were introduced to another senior member of the Baltimore Police Department by the name of Will Lajewski. Officer Lajewski would do all of our training and fieldwork. Will was part dog himself and I am sure the dogs knew this. They would do anything Will would have required of them. Will was knowledgeable and as helpful as anyone could be in all aspects of our training. Every member of the Baltimore Police Department that was involved with dog training went to Will for help or advice when they needed him and he was always willing to help everyone.

We first arrived at the training area, which was a United States government storage area for raw material that was well fenced and patrolled by a security force.

There was a group of Baltimore Police Department officers there as well in a refresher course. The officers entered the classroom we were in with their dogs. One of the officers was handling a very large and nasty looking Rottweiler K-9. Sergeant Knott told me to pet the dog. I walked over to the Rotty and started to pet him. The dog growled like hell and I told the Sergeant it was a nice dog and I stepped back. The Sergeant told me to pet the dog again, so I did, and again the dog growled. I later learned that anytime someone would approach that dog, it would growl. The joke was on me that day but it also showed them I was not nervous or jumpy around the growling dog. Some other people were not nearly as calm with the dogs.

The Department advised us we were assigned to go the Aberdeen Training facility to pick up our assigned dogs. We all went there in our separate vehicles and arrived at the base together. At this time, we were introduced to some civilian employees and soldiers who worked with the United States Army dogs. Our initial conversation with them showed how dedicated to the program these people were and that they all loved the dogs.

When they brought the dogs out to us, our group was standing on a hill with a large field to our front. There were four large wooden boxes which were big enough to hold a man in a bent over position in the field. To our left, two men appeared holding large German Shepherds on leashes. They proceeded to the center of the field and stopped after alerting the dogs to search. One dog went into the area where the large boxes were and alerted on a box. A signal was given and a man broke out of the box and attempted to run away. In a matter of seconds, the dog caught him with his teeth and held him for the handler. The second dog was also let loose and ran the same exercise with the same results. I was amazed at how well the dogs worked and how well they behaved when told to release. They were obviously well trained and disciplined.

We were then introduced to our assigned K-9, and given instructions on how to care for them until school on the following day. We returned to the motel and kept the dogs on leashes at all times. My dog was a black faced, tall and thin male. He was a great looking dog that seemed to be friendly and craved attention as most of the other dogs did. His name was Baretta.

When a dog had a litter of puppies there, each litter was assigned a letter. All of the dogs in that litters names started with the letter B. He was named Baretta after the Italian pistol. Krug has a small female Shepard named Jicky and Curry had a male named Crow.

I had a few beers and went to sleep. The next

morning when I awoke I found Baretta had chewed up one of my shoes. He had also gnawed on the front of the couch. I located the Holiday Inn Hotel manager and advised him of what had happened in his room. I was relieved when he advised me not to be concerned as he was leaving his job soon and he would take care of the problem for me. True to his word when I returned to the room at the end of the day all was in order and the dog never bothered another thing. I always thought too much was expected from a dog that was born in a kennel on an army base. They were kept in confined areas with hundreds of other dogs and had little exposure to the things that occurred in our everyday life like homes, bikes and kids.

The dogs we received from the United States Army were from the Biosensor Research Program. This program was created by the United States Army to provide security dogs for all the branches of the armed forces. They traveled the world over to find breeding stock for these dogs and spared no expense in their breeding and training. It was all very impressive to be a part of.

We soon had a regular schedule with the dog training. Baretta was very good in all aspects of the training and was the best explosive detector dog by far in his class. I would bring him to an explosive scent and praise him. Then I would hide the explosive and let him find it. When he did, he would receive high amounts of praise from me so he knew he was doing a good job. This of course had him crave more positive attention and he would find the next explosive with ease.

During the training, we were required to walk a beat in the City of Baltimore with another K-9 handler of the police department. While walking a beat with my assigned partner, a purse snatching happened fairly close to us in a park. As soon as the officer I was paired up with received the radio transmission, we started moving in the direction of the incident. Within seconds, about eight mounted police officers on horseback galloped by like a cavalry charge. A short time later, we saw that they had caught the desperado and closed the case. I was advised later that the horsemen were just deploying at their assigned post when the crime occurred and they went into action.

On another occasion, an older woman approached me while she was walking on the sidewalk and handed me a package wrapped in aluminum foil. It was about eight inches long, four inches wide and two inches thick. She stated she was ready for any muggings. Upon unwrapping the package, I found she was carrying a brick to defend herself. Obviously, life in Baltimore was tough. She had to be sixty-five years old.

On another day, I was working with a black member of the Baltimore Police Department. His dog was the neatest and cleanest K-9 I had ever seen. When we were on patrol together, he would stop and comb the dog to make sure he looked good and he always talked to the dog with much affection. I was impressed by the way he treated his dog and the love he had for him. The men of the Baltimore Police Department treated us very well and went out of their way to help us all the time.

I eventually introduced myself to the Maryland State Police and I had an opportunity to ride patrol with the K-9 unit that was assigned to the Baltimore Washington International Airport (BWI). At times, Baretta and I assisted them in searching aircraft that had received bomb threats. After working with members of that department, I felt the station and their Troopers could have been moved to New York and it would have functioned as well as the NYSP did. The Maryland Troopers, especially James Gallion of the State Police K-9 unit went out their way to help us out.

While we were in Baltimore for the training detail the Baltimore Police lost a patrolman in a sniping incident. A sniper was shooting and killing people and one of their men died of a gunshot wound as a result of the incident. The Sergeant in charge of the K-9 training advised me the best thing we could do would be to attend the service in uniform to show some respect for their fallen member.

Prior to the funeral detail, we had to enter the Headquarters of the Baltimore Police Department. The sergeant looked us over and asked, "Where are your badges?" I told him we did not wear badges on our uniforms in New York. He then asked if I even had a badge. I advised him we carried badges in our pockets. His reply was "OK put it on your shirt." We put our badges on our shirts and entered the Baltimore Police Headquarters. That afternoon we attended the funeral service and everything went as well as could be expected. The next day we were back in training.

Training with the K-9's involved a lot of walking. We even had some night training to do tracking with the dogs. This was critical in missing person cases. The dogs would follow the tracks and scents of a person to find them. On one day, I would lay a track for the other dogs. On another day, it would be my turn to wear a bite sleeve and hide in the hopes that the dog would find me. All of the training showed me how smart the dogs were.

Many of the exercises we used in training were difficult and strenuous to perform, such as climbing a ladder with the dog on your shoulders. We searched buildings and wooded areas for men that were hiding.

The dogs would alert on the men and attack their bite sleeves.

The latter weeks of training were devoted to explosives and teaching Baretta what he was going to do at the training facilities for the Olympics games. My dog was the best in the class and took to explosives training like a duck to water. I learned how to get him more excited by talking to him as he worked and he would sometimes get so excited he would give me a playful bite! One thing I thought we might have trouble with was the way we were training the dogs to alert when they discovered an explosive. The Baltimore Police Department would let the dog attack the source of the scent. This would involve the dog attacking the box, bag or whatever container the explosive was in. Obviously, this was a dangerous method. The Maryland State Police method of training involved the dog sitting when he obtained the scent and waiting for his reward for finding the hit. This method was much safer because the dog did not disturb the device and therefore would not risk setting off the explosive material. I was confident that my dog could do this and I trained him to do the sit alert without any problem. When the training was almost complete, we went to the army base and demonstrated the dogs for the head of the military unit that we had obtained the dogs from. I was advised he was very impressed with the way my dog worked.

The training was not only for the dogs; it was for the handlers too. I had to learn to read what the dog was doing and thinking. From the first day of training with Baretta until his untimely death, we developed quite a bond. I always felt as if I had ended up with the best K9 New York had. Baretta was part of our family. He assimilated into my life with my wife Blanche and four small children. He let my kids drag him around by the collar without fear, and would fiercely protect them from unwanted guests, and a few wanted ones.

When we finished the school at Baltimore Baretta and I returned to New York and I demonstrated my dog for Sergeant Hornberger. He was very impressed at the way Baretta worked and agreed that my dog was the best of the three New York K-9's. The Division issued me a pager and put me on call twenty-four hours a day. I had been assigned to the bomb section for five years before getting Baretta but I quickly found that his presence made the job much easier for me.

The Bomb on the Bridge

One of the calls I had with Baretta began in the early morning hours of May 27, 1977. I was at my residence and I was notified by phone to report to the City of Amsterdam. On my way up to Amsterdam, I was advised

24

through the radio to see the Amsterdam Sergeant at the bridge going into the city. When I got to the scene, I found all traffic stopped in both directions. Sergeant Hornberger briefed me on what had occurred. I was told that two very sharp Amsterdam Police Department members in uniform on patrol had stopped a vehicle with two license plates displayed. One was on top of the other. The vehicle was occupied by four males, each wearing two sets of clothing, one on top of the other. When the officers got the four subjects out of the vehicle they noticed a small pool of liquid on the floor of the vehicle which evidently spilled from a small bottle (approximately four oz.). After the patrolmen notified the dispatcher and relayed the information of the stop through the radio, the dispatcher notified the patrol they had a hit for a wanted subject on the car from another police department in western NY. The alert was advising them to be careful approaching the occupants as they were known burglars who worked with explosives.

Sergeant Hornberger wanted me to use the dog on the vehicle and check it for explosives. When I arrived on the scene I let the dog out and talked to him for a moment before I led him to the stopped vehicle. When we were about three feet away from the car, the dog stopped and alerted on the vehicle. It was one of the best alerts he ever gave me. I took him further away after a few minutes I released the dog and he went right back to the vehicle and indicated another alert by sitting. I advised Sergeant Hornberger that the dog and I were sure we had an explosive present in the vehicle. We discussed what our next step should be.

Explosives in this condition are very unstable and dangerous to handle. After a short time, the Sergeant decided to remove the floor mat that had the liquid on it from the car and burn the liquid in place. At this point we were the only two persons on the bridge. Sergeant Hornberger found homemade electric blasting caps in the vehicle and we decided to test one. I dropped the blasting cap over the side of the bridge letting it dangle about ten feet down while holding the end of the leg wire. I used a six-volt radar light battery to connect the wire for power and the blasting cap fired as good as a store bought one would have. We then burned the liquid explosive at the scene by setting it on fire.

After the bridge was clear and we were no longer needed on the scene we left. We took a very small sample of the liquid explosive to Division Headquarters in Albany and a lab man was called in to identify the sample. He confirmed the chemical as Nitro-Glycerin. I talked to another Lab man about another case he had in the past with Nitro-Glycerin and he told me one of the recommended field test for nitro was to place a drop on a steel surface and strike it with a hammer. While performing this test he literally blew the head off the hammer. He said that made him think the test was a little too much.

Olympic Security

After we returned to New York from training, one of the jobs waiting for us was providing security for athletes training for the 1975 Olympic Summer Games. The games were scheduled to take place in Montreal, a short distance north of Plattsburgh, New York. Plattsburgh was the training area for the American Team and the New York State Police were in charge of security for the detail. The dogs were assigned to check people and baggage entering and leaving the training area for explosives. At times I felt the security we provided was way too much, but one time we escorted the athletes to the border of Canada and we had about five marked state police units and one helicopter. The Royal Canadian Mounted police waited to meet us with twenty cars and three helicopters. It was then I decided that our security was not over the top at all.

Overall, the job went well and we enjoyed working on that detail. While training for the detail, we used multi-story dorm buildings. Two handlers would go ahead and put out samples of explosives on the first floor. I would then enter that floor and attempt to locate the sample with

Baretta. While I was searching, the other men went on to the next floor putting out new samples. In this manner we would continue to do the entire building. Although it sounds very simple it was hard work and exhausting for the dogs. There was no dog on that detail that would come close to mine in the number of finds and hours worked. Baretta was a hard worker and very efficient.

Sniper on the Second Floor

On October 30, 1976, I was working an afternoon shift and the activity was routine. It had just gotten dark and I had stopped an eighteen-wheel tractor-trailer which was missing a truck mileage plate (TMT) issued by the state tax department. The TMT plate was required on all trucks over eighteen thousand pounds. As I was inspecting the truck, I located an unregistered hidden handgun. I placed the driver under arrest and placed him in the troop vehicle for transportation to the nearest State Police station, which in this case was in Saratoga.

When I arrived at the station, the deskman activated the door buzzer to unlock the door and allowed the trucker and I access to the building. The desk Trooper advised that Investigator Toby Campbell was the duty detective and by regulations, I was required to notify the BCI of the felony arrest. I contacted Investigator Campbell at his residence and he advised me he was on his way in. I began to process the truck driver taking his fingerprints and filling out the arrest report. By the time Investigator Campbell entered the station I had most of the required processing work complete. I had worked with Investigator Campbell in other areas and he was known as a hard worker and had the smarts to do what was required of him. While completing the processing, the desk officer came back into the area we were in and advised that a local city Police Department was involved in an active shooting and they were requesting assistance.

I let the investigator know that I wanted to respond to assist the other police agency. He told me to go and he would finish processing the gun case. I got in the troop car and advised Baretta to hang on as we were going for a ride and we flew to the city of Mechanicville. Upon entering the city, it was easy to find the area of the shooting because everyone in the city was on their porch looking down the road toward the direction of the incident. I could hear the gunshots as I approached the area. The shooter was firing very rapid eight round bursts. I stopped the car once and got out but I did not see anything. I then reentered the vehicle and went about two more blocks and it appeared as if all hell broke loose. I could see muzzle flashes from a large caliber weapon coming out of a second floor window and it was almost directly in front of me. Although I found myself on the ground next to the

29

car, I could not remember getting out of the car.

Within a minute, another trooper slid in next to me as if he was sliding into second base. He ended up beside me next to my car. Trooper Bill Khachadourian and I worked in the same station and were good friends. Within a couple of minutes, another man joined us with the same type of slide that Bill had used. The man was a paramedic who wanted to let us know that the bullets from the shooter's gun were passing through vehicles and they would offer us little or no protection from the gunfire. I thanked him and told him get the hell out of the area. Bill suggested we run across the road to the shooters building. I told him to wait until the shooter stops shooting and while he was reloading, we could run. Bill agreed. I told him to get ready and as soon as he stopped shooting, I said, "Let's go!" We no sooner left the cover of the vehicle, and the subject started shooting again and went through eight rounds in a matter of a few seconds. We both got to the side of a brick building and Bill said, "I'm not listening to anything you have to say about this guy." We both laughed like hell.

From our new position, we worked our way into the shooter's building and I found myself in the kitchen of the apartment directly under the shooter. I saw a telephone on the wall and decided to contact Troop Headquarters because I was thinking they might want to know what we were up to. I dialed the number for my Sergeant (Wayne Bennett). He answered and before I could tell him who was calling, the shooter let loose with 8 more rounds right above us. Sergeant Bennett asked, "Is that the bad guy shooting". I replied in the affirmative. He told me to be careful and I briefed him on what was going on with myself and Bill. We then assisted two Investigators from the Mechanicsville city Police Department to get the innocent people to leave the apartment below the one housing the shooter.

After we cleared that apartment, about five of us, Khachadourian, two investigators from the city Police Department, myself and one other man wearing a plain shirt with a small badge pinned to it moved towards the shooter's apartment. Just as we started to change positions, we smelled a very bad odor in the hall. I asked the group, "What the hell is that smell?" One of the officers replied, "It's me, I crawled through a large pile of dog shit on my way here." We all started up the stairs to the shooter's apartment. He was one floor above us.

After we went up a few steps, Bill touched my arm to get my attention and when I looked at him, he pointed at the wall in the hallway above us. I looked up and as I watched a group of bullet holes was visible in the wall and new ones appeared as we stood there. These rounds were passing above us and were being fired by the police

31

shooting back at the bad guy from across the street. I learned later that some of police from outside the city had broken into a gun store and were using the inventory from the store to engage the shooter.

When we tried to enter the apartment of the shooter, the door would not budge. We later learned, the shooter pushed the refrigerator over on its side and wedged it against the door to prevent our entry. One of the city investigators drew his pistol and fired five or six shots through the wall in an attempt to stop the shooting. The man beside me wearing the badge on his shirt started to jump around so badly I thought he was shot. I grabbed him and asked him if he was all right he answered in the affirmative. I then glanced at Bill and when I looked back, that guy was gone and I never saw him again. The rest of us then went back down the steps and re-entered the first floor apartment. There was a strange young man standing in the kitchen. One of the detectives questioned him and learned he was just a passerby. He was thrown out and told not to come back. We all started to look the area over for another entrance or solution to the problem.

At this time, I was in the back of the building and I observed a man and a woman in the apartment next to the shooters. They were on the second floor trying to exit the building. I encouraged them to get out as soon as possible. The man came down a ladder and hit the ground a running. A few seconds later, the woman tried to come down, but she fell all the way down and hit with a very loud noise. I broke from my cover and ran over to her on the ground with the intention of picking her up and getting her to a safe area. I was in the open and directly below the shooter's apartment. When I looked down at the woman, I realized I could not pick her up, as she had to weigh well over two hundred pounds. I was very reluctant to holster my revolver, as all the bad guy had to do was look out his back window and I was a sitting duck standing there with the woman. I asked her if she could walk she replied, "I don't think so". I then asked her if she could crawl and she replied, "I think so". I told her to go quickly and she started crawling at high speed toward the corner with me walking beside her and covering the bad guy's window with my service revolver.

After this incident I went back to the front of the building and nothing had changed. The shooting had not let up from both directions. Across the street and directly in front of Joyce's Log Cabin Restaurant, someone had parked a station wagon. I could see the shooter used it as a target for awhile. I could see the bullets go in on one side of the car and come out the other. The responding police officers were still returning fire. I returned to the rear of the building. I could see Trooper Powers in the corner of a lot about 100 feet away from the building with other police officers that were not visible.

The siege went on for about two or three hours. While gunfire was still coming from across the street, I heard the shooter shouting that he wanted to surrender. I was back in the front part of the building when I heard him. I then went to the rear of the building and I could still hear him at times. I then walked to the lot near his apartment and yelled put down your gun and come out. He stated, "Don't shoot me". I replied "I won't shoot you, come out now". At the time I was thinking, I applied to go to the hostage negotiating school, but the Division refused my request. Now here I was, talking this guy out of his apartment. I watched him as he came out holding his hands up. I told him not to move and to keep his hands up.

Troopers were coming out of everywhere to assist me in the arrest. Trooper Gundrum left his perch in the corner and came over to say "hello". I remained in place and ordered the subject to come down the ladder from his rear patio. When he put his hands down to grip the ladder someone yelled, "put your hands up" and he complied very quickly. I then advised him to continue down. The minute he touched the ground we were on him like stink on shit.

I then realized the police in the front of the building

were still shooting at the second floor apartment, the one that the bad guy had been in. I took my gun sight off the K-5 area (the center mass of the chest) of the shooter and went to the front of the building. I yelled cease-fire the guy is in custody as loud as I could. We did not have portable radios to communicate with each other at that time. A large amount of State Troopers began to come out including some Commissioned Officers. Captain George Abare advised me to make sure I secured the room in the building that the shooter had been using. It was a crime scene. He said he wanted me in there before the firemen to protect the evidence and prevent it all from being washed away. The building had caught fire in the last hour of the incident and was starting to burn pretty good.

I went into the entrance of the apartment with the firemen. Soon I located the room the muzzle flashes had been coming out of and entered it. The floor in the room had at least a foot of water on it. I got a fireman in the hall to chop a hole in the floor to give the water someplace to go. All I was wearing on my feet was dress shoes and they were soaked. After the State Police crime scene identification men got to the room, we started to collect the evidence involved in the case. I was designated as the member to handle all of the firearms. The shooter had ten long guns in the room. Most of them were on the bed. As I picked up one long gun, an M1 30.06 Garand, I saw it was the same weapon I carried in the United States

Marine corps. I noticed the gun had the combat sight setting marked in red and I realized that this was the weapon that was doing most of the shooting. I was amazed that I did not recognize it from the ejection noise it made before a new clip was loaded.

A couple of shotguns also were used in the shooting. One of the officers was shot in the face with a shotgun. Another officer had been hit in the head most likely by the M1. He died on the spot. I learned later he was only on the job for three months. I had seen him earlier in the evening on his back on the sidewalk with a severe head wound. While he lay there dead, a reporter started to film him up close. I got mad as hell thinking the video would be seen by his friends and family. I yelled to Investigator Bruce Arnold who I had spotted close to the cameraman to stop him from filming. He waved me off and then I realized the Investigator had most likely requested the reporter take the picture as evidence for the criminal investigation. Bruce was an old friend of mine. We had both served on the Capitol Police in Albany in 1963 before we joined the New York State Police. He had been one of the first narcotics investigators assigned to "G" troop. Kenyon William Pruyn, age 32, killed 2 people and wounded 9 others on that day. He would receive a sentence of 25 years to life for his crimes.

I found a working phone and called my wife to let

her know everything was OK and I would be home as soon as possible. The detail returned to Loudonville Troop Headquarters and after a few short memos we were let go to an off duty status. Arriving home I found my wife was waiting up for me. She had to know everything that occurred and after a short conversation we went to bed. I tried to sleep, but my body was still running on pure adrenalin, so I got out of bed and went out to have a cup of coffee. This incident was the most involved case that I ever had and I was pretty happy about the way it turned out.

After the incident was over Capt. George Abare put my name in for a very high award. William Khachadourian was also recommended for the same award. There came a time when the Keough and Khachadourian families were invited to a very nice awards dinner in Yonkers, New York to be honored. We spent the night at a hotel as guests of the group that had given us the award. My wife enjoyed herself a lot. She was away from the kids for an adult night out.

Serial Burglar in Clifton Park

Another incident I was involved in at about the same time as the shootout in Mechanicville, happened when I was conducting burglary investigations in the Clifton Park area. A thief was entering homes while the owners were working or otherwise occupied stealing various items. I received a complaint from the Loudonville Dispatcher of a burglary in the town of Clifton Park on State route 146. I drove to the location and interviewed the owner. He showed me where the burglar had entered a cellar window. I checked the area around the window for fingerprints and I could not find any sign of a print anywhere. I asked him if it would be possible for him to check the wooded area behind his house because many burglars hide things in the woods behind the houses they enter and return later to get the loot.

I then went outside with the owner and explained to him that I had another assignment to talk to a group of Cub Scouts about my dog. I then went to the Town of Colonie to speak to a large group of cub scouts. I had stopped at a sporting goods store and picked up a neck scarf and cub scouts tie holder for Baretta to wear. As expected, the children loved the dog and they all wanted to pet him at the same time. After I finished the assignment, I returned to my patrol area.

Shortly after returning to my post, Dispatch advised me to contact my burglary complainant. When I called the man who had reported the burglary, he advised me he had found his property in the woods behind the house. I advised him to leave the property alone for now and I would call him right back. I then contacted the duty

Bureau of Criminal Investigation (BCI) man and advised him of what I had. He told me to have the guy pick up his property because he wasn't able to come in and work the case. I did not want to do it but had no choice in the matter. I contacted the complainant and advised him to return his property to his residence.

I drove to the area where the property was found and located a spot where I could park the marked State Police unit and observe the area without being seen. I located an area in a sand pit just off the road but I was worried that the traffic on state route 146 might light up the decals on my car. I contacted Trooper Tommy Guttridge on the troop radio and asked him to run by and see if he could see the decals of my vehicle, he replied that he would be there soon. I knew his location and that he would be coming from the east and I started to watch for him. Within a few minutes, he comes by and I can spot his car but also on the other side of the highway, I see a good-sized man standing alongside of the road with a large flashlight.

I contact Guttridge on the troop car radio and inquire as to the man standing off the road. He advises he was not able to see the guy. I told him to return pick the guy up and bring him to me. Trooper Guttridge pulls up with the man in his car. I dismount from my vehicle and approached the guy. In his pants pocket I found a large screwdriver in one pocket and a pair of socks in the other. He also had socks on his feet so I knew he was a good suspect for the burglary. I had arrested burglars who carried socks to put over their hands when they were doing a job. Add to that the fact that a large screwdriver is one of the most common burglar tools used.

His answers to questions as to why he was in that area and what he was doing were evasive, so I transported the subject to the station in Saratoga and again contacted the BCI Investigator. This time he advised he was on his way in and arrived at the station soon after. I assisted with the interview of the subject. He did not admit guilt and kept insisting he was not guilty of anything. The investigator advised he would continue the case the next day and the subject was interviewed on the following day. The man was arrested for thirty burglaries and thousands of dollars in property was recovered.

Trooper Guttridge and myself each received a letter from the Troop Commander telling us we did a nice job. All the BCI men involved in the case got letters of Commendation from the Superintendent of State Police. That is the way the State Police Uniform Troopers were treated. We always come in second place to the BCI. Relative to this case, I knew we had a lot of luck and very possibly, we might have ended with no arrest if things had gone a little different.

Burglary in Town of Halfmoon

Another case Guttridge and I worked was in the town of Halfmoon. I was investigating the burglary of a supermarket in the Town of Halfmoon. I was doing interviews in the area the day of the report and a local woman told me her dog had bitten a young man in her yard behind the supermarket. The bite had occurred at a very late hour and the subject bitten was known to me as a thief. I arrested him in the past for larcenies. When I interviewed the subject, he admitted to nothing although I believed he was lying. The case was stalled. I contacted a BCI member from the Saratoga Station for assistance. He told me to arrange a lie detector test. I scheduled the test and the subject agreed to come in. The investigator that conducted the test was a good hard-working man and did his best but the test was inconclusive. Two days later Guttridge and I were riding night patrol (11PM to 7AM) and we checked the market. We caught the thief coming out of the woods behind the market carrying the cases of beer he had stolen in the burglary. He was hiding them in the woods and coming back later for them. We arrested the man after a short foot race and placed him in the troop car. He admitted to the earlier theft.

The reason he had defeated the last test was that I

did not give the investigator enough information about the case. One of the things that he did when he entered the market during theft was that he would remove the molding around the entry door and replace it when he was done so there was no entry marks evident on the door jams or windows. We did not have much information on what was taken because of the large inventory of goods in the store. The lack of information on the burglary made it all the harder to close the case with the lie detector test. That did not stop me from busting the investigator's balls about us solving his case without him.

A Homicide in Saratoga

A homicide case I was involved with happened in the Saratoga area. I had taken my assigned vehicle, a four-wheel drive truck, to the radio shop in Schenectady to have the radio repaired. While at Leonard Communications on Crane Street in the city as they were completing the radio repair, I heard a radio transmission from a BCI unit in Saratoga advising Dispatch he was chasing a vehicle that was flagged as a "File 12", wanted person. The occupant was wanted for murder.

I took my Vehicle from the repair shop and headed to Saratoga thinking I was too far away and the chase would be over before I got there. Within about ten minutes, I arrive at the scene where the bad guy's car ran off the road in a development and I saw Investigator David Foster on foot nearby. He entered a building and came out waving me in. I dismounted the vehicle and joined Dave in the hallway of the basement apartment. He whispered to me that the women in that apartment just told him the guy was in her house. Dave told me to guard the apartment while he rounded up the other BCI men. I had my K-9 on a leash in the hall when Dave headed out the door. I looked at the door to the apartment the bad guy was in and I could see that the door was made of the thinnest wood they could use and I realized I could put my fist thru it. Dave returned with about six BCI men.

I excused myself to put Baretta in the Troop car. There was a baby and a young woman in the apartment and I did not want the dog to accidently bite someone. When I returned, the young women had exited the apartment. I understand that while I was gone, one of the BCI men dragged her out and she was very upset that her child was still inside with the killer. I tried to do my best to calm her down and convince her that staying outside was the best thing to do. I no sooner said that when the bad guy fired off a round inside of the apartment. The mother asked what that was and I told her I did not know. She attempted to push past me because she realized it was a gunshot in the same apartment her baby was in, and I stopped her. I explained to her that I could not let her pass by me and if I had to, I would force her to the ground and hold her until this thing was over for her safety. I got her to agree to come outside with me. I thought it would get her out of range and might calm her down. I brought her out of the building and a short distance later, I spotted a cop from the Scotia police department that I knew and I asked him to take care of her and I went back to the apartment.

Arriving back at the building, I found the bad guy shot himself in the head. I entered the kitchen and picked up the diaper bag, milk and other things the baby needed. I passed a BCI man who was on his way to return the baby to his mother. I believed that woman would hate Troopers for the rest of her life. We kept her from her child at a very stressful time. The fact that we split the mother and child at this scene seemed cruel, but the moment we got her from the apartment, we reduced our hostages by fifty percent and in that way, it made sense. The poor woman's apartment was left a mess. Gore and blood that comes from a head wound was all over the room the man killed himself in and all the flash bulbs and paper littered the crime scene from the investigation.

Breaking Down Doors

One of my other partners on the night patrol in Guilderland was Trooper Tim Fischer. We had some great times and made many good arrests. Tim became a

K-9 officer after Baretta had died. One night, we were checking a motel on the 11PM to 7AM shift and I checked a vehicle parked in an area where people did not normally park. A routine file check on the vehicle showed the occupant came back as a wanted person. The crime was not that serious but we decided to look into it and I approached the door of the motel room where the man was staying. We knocked on the door and announced our presence to no avail. The lights were on in the room and the TV was blaring.

We then tried the door and it opened but caught on the chain lock. At this time Fischer yells "GUN!", so I drew my gun and I see a man walking toward the door with a handgun pointed in our direction. I yell as loud as I can "POLICE PUT THE GUN DOWN!" The guy in the room says, "show me your badge." I yell, "PUT THE GUN DOWN NOW". Once again, he says he wants to see my badge. Most people do not realize Troopers in New York do not display badges on their uniforms. We carry badges, but they are in a case in our pocket and I was not about to put my gun down to look for the badge. At this time, I see the man in the crack of the door trying to look at us. I lunged at the door which broke the chain holding it partly open. The door opens and knocks the gun from the man's hand. I ended up on top of the guy on the floor and Fischer yelled that he has secured the gun. The man was angry with us that we were in his room uninvited. He knew nothing about the vehicle that was parked in front because it was not his car. We later had that car towed and arrested the person who was wanted when he came to pick it up.

We contact Zone One Headquarters to report the incident to our boss. A Zone Sergeant and the Zone Commander (a Lieutenant) came to the scene. In the mean time we found out the man from the hotel room was deaf and could not hear us pounding on the door. His hearing aids were in plain sight on the nightstand. The Lieutenant was a good man. He told us he was glad to see we were doing our job and not sleeping in the bushes. He went on to say that I might have to explain what happened to the Troop Commander (Bennett) though. Fischer and I went to the troop car and we started laughing so hard we were actually crying. The Lieutenant did not know it, but when current Troop Commander Bennett was a sergeant, he and I had to see the then Troop Commander relative to breaking into another motel room in Latham.

That door incident involved a man in a Latham motel on the Latham traffic circle. We received a teletype message from "A" Troop (Buffalo) area advising our station that an escaped prisoner from Attica prison was located at the motel. I was at the scene with the Troop Commander (then Sergeant Bennett) and I tried to see if the door was closed or open. The room was not visible from our position and we did not want to show the marked police car, so we requested an unmarked troop car ride by and check the room. The unmarked patrol soon arrived and drove by the room. The Trooper in the unmarked car told us the door was open. We then went up the side of the building to the room. When we got in front of the room, I saw the door was shut tight. I advised Sergeant Bennett and he told me to try the door. I did as instructed. As soon as I touched the doorknob, the curtain flew open and the occupant of the room was staring right in my face. No way to hide, I crashed through the door with my dog and we found ourselves in the motel room. The man in the room surrendered right off, but the woman ran into the bathroom and of course I followed her in. I think she was trying to escape through the showerhead! She also surrendered. When the matter was straightened out, we discovered the man was the brother of the escaped prisoner and was also a convicted felon. Without a reason to arrest the man we left after letting the motel manager know the door needed to be fixed.

The next day when I reported to work, Sergeant Bennett was waiting for me. As soon as he could, he advised me that both of us had to see the Troop Commander. The Major was interested in what went on during our last shift. He was concerned as to why the motel gave him a bill for three hundred dollars for a new door. We explained and all was forgiven. Just as I thought, Troop Commander Bennett never asked to see me about the Guilderland incident.

Keough and Fischer

Fischer and I had a few other cases that were pretty good. One night we were standing alongside of the Thruway exit at Schenectady and a car pulled up to the toll barrier with a temporary registration tag. I could see the tag was for a Japanese import, but it was displayed on a Pontiac. I began a conversation with the driver who has a thick Spanish accent but was speaking English fairly well. I also notice that the vehicle behind him was also a Pontiac with a Spanish looking person at the wheel. They were both wearing pork pie hats. We flagged the second vehicle operator to the side of the road. Fischer and I start to talk to the operators. As the incident went on, we discovered the first car was a stolen vehicle and the second vehicle contained a Vehicle Identification Number (VIN) plate off a third vehicle. Possession of a VIN plate was a felony. We arrested the two of them and sent them to Albany County jail after visiting a town judge for arraignment.

While we were transporting them and processing them at the State Police station they both "forgot" how to speak English and refused to talk to us. The next day one

48

of the defendants called me on the phone from the county jail and wanted to talk about his case. It was amazing but his English improved with one night in jail. I told him I could not understand him, but if he remained at the county jail long enough, he would learn the English language and I would be able to understand him better. I had two more calls from him and on the last one he told me he was going to bring a lawyer with him. I told him he should bring two lawyers as they would do a better job than one.

At the same exit area of the Thruway, Fischer and I were out of the car talking to the toll collector when a car went through the toll and entered the Thruway. As soon as he got on the ramp, he hit a large light pole and came to a stop. We went over to help and the first thing I noticed was the passenger door was crushed. The passenger was a pretty blond with a very short mini skirt on. I knew instantly she would have to climb over the console to exit the vehicle, so I hurried around the car to help the poor girl in the mini skirt climb out. Fischer was right in my spot and would not move out of the way...no matter how hard I pushed him.

That same night, three young men stopped at our checkpoint and when they opened up the glove compartment, a very large pistol was visible. I shouted "GUN" to Fischer and drew my revolver. We discovered that the gun was a pellet pistol. The driver's license was not in order so we called the owner to come get the vehicle. She came, but was very annoyed with us.

When Fischer and I were riding night patrol in Guilderland, there were many commercial burglaries of flower shops, bars and other small businesses at that time. One night we spotted two subjects crossing route 20 on foot in an area that had very little foot traffic at that time of night. Fischer pulled up beside them and I got out to interview them. As I approached the one guy, I could see he had a flashlight and a large screw driver hanging out of his pocket. My interview revealed that both subjects did not live in the area they were in and were evasive about what they were doing there. The second subject also had tools that could be used in the commission of a burglary.

We transported both subjects to State police Guilderland station and contacted the on duty BCI man. The on call man was Investigator Jim Horton who responded. He agreed with us as to the subject's evasiveness. After he interrogated the subjects, we were able to close seven of our commercial burglaries and put a stop to any new burglaries (of the same type). Jim Horton was an exceptional Investigator who did very efficient work in his job assignment.

Another caper that Fischer and I were involved with was when we had a call about gunshots in a housing area. We located the address given and dismounted from our troop car. We walked up to the building and looked into the apartment. It was easy to do because the front door was torn off the building and was lying on the sidewalk. We walked into the apartment and there were three young men inside. Fischer came in behind me and said "GUN". I turned and saw him pick up a revolver from the floor. The gun smelled of being fired recently and we located a bullet hole in the wall. After being advised of their rights, they admitted to possession of the gun. A check with the dispatcher showed the gun was stolen somewhere in a northern county of New York State. We arrested the subjects transported them to the station and contacted the BCI as the case was a felony. The men were in possession of a loaded handgun and stolen property.

On patrol with Trooper Tim Fischer once, we got a request from the Massachusetts State Police to interview a man at the emergency room of the Albany Medical Center hospital. They believed the man was involved in an attempted homicide that occurred in Massachusetts and that he was the perpetrator of the incident. We patrolled to the Medical Center and find the man has been admitted for emergency surgery because of a severe laceration to his hand. We interviewed the doctor involved in the case and advised him that the patient is a suspect in an attempted murder case. We told the doctor that in order to guard him, we would like to have at least one of us in the room while he was being operated on. The guy was only getting a local anesthesia and the operating room had more than one exit. The doctor was very helpful he advised me the inside man would have to wear a gown. I told him fine, could we get one in Fischer's size.

After the operation started, Fischer came out to speak with me and when he started talking, I did not know who he was because he was so covered. All I could see was his eyes. That struck me as very funny. When the guy came out of the operating room after the surgery, we interviewed him as per the request from the Massachusetts State Police. We acted like we knew all about it, but asked him to give us his version and he seemed very truthful. They sent another Trooper to relieve us and we contacted the Massachusetts State Police to let them know what we learned from the subject. They were pleased with our results.

Keough and McGreevy

I also spent many nights riding with Jerry McGreevy as my patrol partner. He would eventually become my Zone Sergeant/supervisor in later years before transferring to another station. We became good friends many years ago and still are to this day. I had my K-9 Baretta when we rode night patrol together. Our patrol was in most cases very busy and that was what we both liked.

One of our capers took place in Guilderland Center. As we drove south on Route 146 we noticed a man standing behind a closed gin mill in a small shopping plaza on the right side of the road. It was 5 am. I turned into the lot in front of the bar and shut the car lights off. I slowly drove around to the rear of the building and we came right up behind the man. He had a small crowbar and was prying at the rear locked door of the bar. I exited the vehicle with Baretta. The dog was barking and ready to bite the desperado. The man surrendered right off and dropped a small bag he was carrying. Upon examining the bag, we found it contained a full set of tools for the local burglar. There was a screwdriver, crowbar, hammer, mask and gloves. We charged him with possession of burglar tools and attempted burglary. The man was also extremely intoxicated. He was breaking in at 5 am to get some more booze.

Jerry and I had another caper in the same shopping center. This time on the other side of the building. We were riding through Guilderland center and got flagged down by a pedestrian who I knew as the maintenance man for the complex. He reported that he had tried to get a vehicle to move off the lawn but the operator had pulled out a pistol and threatened to shoot him. We pulled up close to the vehicle, which was a small van. We dismounted very quietly and approached. Jerry took the right side and I approached on the left. We then yelled, "State Police" and threw open the sliding door of the van. We found a man and women completely naked having intercourse on the floor of the van (the girl looked great). I grabbed the man by the neck and pulled him from the vehicle and I could say without a doubt he did not have a gun on him. I soon heard Jerry say he found the gun. It was loaded and unregistered so we had some felony charges. After they were transported to the station, we called for a BCI man for the case and he decided to let the female go. She was annoyed with us and did not want to give her name or information but she finally came around and we let her go.

About five years later, I received a call from a State Police crime task force investigator in the center of the state. He asked questions about the man involved in this case. The investigator talking to me was amazed that I remembered it so well. I asked him if he ever arrested

54

anyone in the middle of intercourse. He told me the man was on a wiretap talking to an organized crime member. When they identified the man and ran his name, his criminal record came up with the gun arrest with my name on it.

Another case that Jerry and I had in that complex was a woman who was always getting picked up as a person in need of mental help. At times, she would get annoyed with the police and on one occasion, she bit the Chief of Police of Guilderland. I found out she liked Irish music, so when we picked her up and placed her in the troop car to transport her to the hospital, we would sing Irish songs to her and she would be happy to sing along. Every so often, I would yell, "Duck here comes your mother!", and she would laugh and duck down in the troop car seat. We never had any problems with her after that.

Zone Sergeant Mcgreevy and I had large number of DWI arrests when we were Troopers together. One of them occurred one night on I-87 at the intersection of state route 20. We came upon a vehicle stopped on the pavement on I-87 at the traffic light at route 20. The car was in the middle of the road and the operator was sound asleep behind the wheel. The car was in gear, motor running and the operator's foot was on the brake. There is also another passenger sound asleep lying on the front seat of the vehicle. When this occurred, I was the Trooper in charge, so I tell McGreevy that I am going to open the driver's door, pull the operator out and hand him to Jerry. I will then get in the car and drive it off the road. I was afraid that the car would roll away without me and hit another vehicle on route 20. Somehow, we pulled it off without a hitch. Jerry grabbed the drunk on his feet and I jumped in the car and drove it off the road. The only problem I had was the passenger in the car was also drunk. He woke up and was startled to see me driving the car. The first thing he said was, "Joe, where did you get the mailman's pants?"

One other DWI arrest that Mcgreevy and I handled was on State route 20 at the intersection of Fuller Road in the Town of Guilderland. It involved a very pretty young nurse. We were stopped at a traffic light at the intersection and she was going in the opposite direction. She crossed the lanes of traffic and stopped directly in front of us on the wrong side of the road. Route 20 is a 4-lane highway that is generally very busy both day and night. We initiated a vehicle stop and I got out of the vehicle and approached the operator. I asked the pretty nurse for her license and registration. She opened her very large purse and handed me her bra. I told her we needed to see her license and registration. She then pulled out a bag of marijuana and handed me that. We then arrested her and brought her to the substation. She asked to use the phone and she called her boyfriend who she commenced to chew out blaming him for all of her troubles. When she took the breathalyzer test, she had a very high reading.

Jerry and I had arrested another pretty women one other night. She had broken into her boyfriend's apartment and refused to leave. She also refused to get out when we requested her to leave. At the station, we attempted to fingerprint her and she chose to start a fight with Jerry. I got involved and put her on the floor but she continued to fight me after she was down. When she stopped, we processed her and took her back to her house. The next day as we are getting ready for our shift to start we heard a knock on the door. I open it and there is our pretty girl from the night before sober and clean as can be. She entered the station and started to apologize for the night before. She said, "I'm sorry I made you roll around the floor with me." I told her I did not mind that at all and in fact I rather enjoyed it because she was so pretty. I think she felt better when she left.

On another night with Jerry McGreevy as my partner, we stopped for a coffee at the Dunkin Donuts shop on Western Avenue by the Albany city line. After walking inside the shop, the large front plate glass window of the shop shattered. We turned and ran out the front door and immediately saw off to our right three men that appear to be Arabs and to our left were three

American males around twenty years old. The Arabs were talking to each other and not looking at us at all. The American males were standing in a gin mill parking lot looking at us. We approached and interviewed them as to whether they knew who threw something that shattered the window. They told us nothing. One subject had a very bad attitude, but we could not hold them without evidence, so we release them. Low and behold, they got into their vehicle, which was displaying an expired registration sticker. We stopped the vehicle and issued the proper uniform traffic ticket and towed the vehicle away.

We continued on patrol and about a half hour later I spotted a car making the same turns we were and I noticed it was following us on our patrol. We stopped the vehicle and it turned out it was the same person that we were involved with at the Dunkin Donut Shop. A few more uniform traffic tickets were issued for violations and the subject was released.

We kept the broken window case active. One night, six months after the incident, I happened to stop one of the three men that had been at the shop that night. We arrested him on other charges and he had a change of heart. He told me what happened that night. I obtained the statement from him and went to see the town justice who agreed to issue a felony warrant of arrest charging criminal mischief for our suspect. The following night we were scheduled to go to court with our defendant for the traffic tickets that we wrote the night the window was broken.

We all showed up on time and the defendant was called up to the bench with me. The judge advised me that the defendant was requesting a delay in the case. I told the judge that we would go along with the delay as I had a more important case that we would like to work on. The judge set a new date for the Vehicle & Traffic offenses. We thanked him and then I told the Judge the other case I had to work on was a felony criminal mischief charge for this defendant. We arrested him in the courtroom and took him into custody. I felt great knowing in this matter there was some justice in this world.

Jerry and I had another occasion to get involved with another gentleman who wasn't always so gentle. He was riding a large motorcycle on route 20 and decided to go into the Denny's Restaurant. On the back of the motorcycle was the girl my mother warned me about. When she walked through the restaurant without her boyfriend, a college boy said something to the girl. After she rejoined our hero at their table, she told him about the comment the college kid made. She pointed the boy out as he was getting into his car behind the restaurant to her boyfriend. In defense of the girl's honor, our hero motorcycle man, ran out to the front of the restaurant and waited for the college kid's car to drive out. When the car passed, motorcycle man dove onto the hood of the car and killed the car by stabbing it with a large buck knife through the hood. The car had two other occupants, one of which bailed out and went running off through the field next to the restaurant. Motorcycle man, still on the hood, punched out the windshield.

The operator of the now dead car was crying and not in a very good mood when we arrived. I exited the troop car with the dog on a leash in one hand and a club in the other and motorcycle man surrendered. The complainant was scared to death and refused to sign a complaint, so we had to release him. After a week or so, the young man changed his mind and we did arrest the car killer on a warrant.

On one of my patrols with Jerry McGreevy in the town of Guilderland we had a complaint from a resident who lived near one of the town's water towers. The complaint reported someone was parked in her driveway. On arriving at the scene, we see a lone car with two people in it and they are having intercourse, almost naked. We made noise and gave them plenty of time to get dressed but it did not work. They did not stop and made no attempt to disguise what was going on. We told them they had to go and we would not let them continue.

60

The woman told us she was almost done. About this time, I noticed she was in her fifties and the man was in his twenties. After some more noise, she left.

One afternoon shift I remember was when McGreevy was now a Zone Sergeant and I was working the afternoon shift out of the Guilderland station. He came into the locker room at the beginning of shift change and asked me why I was not ready for work. I was still getting dressed. I asked him what time it was and he told me I was three minutes late. I told him another Zone Sergeant called me about a pending case and I was talking to him on the phone. He had called me twice. Obviously, Jerry did not believe me because he asked me, "What took you so long in the shower?" I didn't answer, so he asked me again, "What took you so long in the shower?" My answer was, "I got to scrubbing my balls and it felt so good I just kept scrubbing and scrubbing." The rest of the guys in the station were howling, they were laughing harder than I ever heard them. Jerry left and at a later time delivered a memo to me from Troop telling me I was bad. I had Sergeants that I knew calling me on the phone and asking if that really happened. Some of them were stationed up to fifty miles away!

Murderer on the Loose

One arrest that I felt very good about was a homicide arrest I made on a notice that was put out on the radio out of Troop Headquarters. When any patrol in the troop gets a serious complaint such as a murder or serious assault, dispatch puts out a radio notice on the case that goes to all the troopers. The information is usually sketchy because the case has not developed yet, but they want the patrols to be aware of the incident so they can assist in the apprehension of the bad guys. I had just checked in on the radio one afternoon and they put an item out of Troop "G" on a homicide that occurred in Rensselaer County, east of Albany. The radio transmission was broken, so I stopped in a Stewart's store to phone the communications section of Troop Headquarters. This was way before the time of cell phones.

The Trooper assigned to dispatch answered the phone. He advised that the State Police was investigating a homicide that had just occurred and a vehicle wanted in the case was seen leaving the crime scene. He gave me the description and color of the vehicle. I thanked him and went back to my car. I started to go east on Route 20 in the direction of the homicide. Within a few minutes, I spotted a vehicle that looked like the one they were looking for. The car was going west, but the traffic was so heavy that I could not see it well enough to confirm if it was the one. I U-turned and started to get closer to it in traffic. I contacted Troop headquarters on the radio and the dispatcher sounded annoyed with me because I just talked to him on the phone. He broadcasted to me that I should report emergency traffic only. I fixed his ass by declaring myself in a "signal 30" status with the before mentioned Vehicle. Signal 30 is given by patrols that have an emergency situation. All patrols must get of the air and pay attention to the Trooper in the Signal 30. Suddenly the dispatcher gives me his complete attention. At that point, he wanted my location, status and everything else. I updated the dispatcher as we continued westbound on Route 20 at about forty miles per hour. The dispatcher advised my nearest backup was fifteen miles away.

I knew the backup Trooper and that this was his very first day on the road in this patrol area. He asked me if it would be all right if he went to Latham at the start of our shift I said sure go ahead. At this point, we were coming to the traffic light at Routes 20 and 146 and the bad guy stopped. I pulled up and stopped behind him. A school bus full of children pulled up and stopped beside him. I was thinking maybe I could approach the guy at the light on foot, but the appearance of the school bus put a stop to that idea. About ten seconds later, a tractor-trailer pulled in behind me and I knew I could not escape now if he started shooting and I was fearful for the safety of the children.

The light changed and the man started moving forward slowly. As I pull up beside him (gun in hand), he would not look at me. We approached the Governor's Motel and I drove close to the side of his car and he quickly turned right into the motel parking lot. He attempted to head back out onto Route 20 and I cut him off. At this point, I saw John Tashjian, a member of the Guilderland police department coming up the hill in front of the motel with a shotgun. I dismounted and went up to the driver's window yelling to the operator "DON'T MOVE OR I WILL KILL YOU." I saw a revolver on the floor of his car as well as spotted brass casings so I knew that the gun is loaded and was possibly fired. As luck would have it, a BCI investigator by the name of Ralph Barbone arrived at the scene and parked close to the bad guy too.

I reached into the car and grabbed the bad guy by the head and pulled him out of the window. As his body was clearing the car, I spotted a holster stuffed in his pants under his shirt. At first, I thought it might have been a small pistol, but when I put my hand on it, I realized it was a dagger. The knife was in it! Also in his front pants pocket there was a large butterfly knife (that opens with the flick of the wrist). He was taken into custody without further incident. I escorted the vehicle, which was loaded, on a tow truck to the State Police East Greenbush station. The defendant was transported separately by a two-man patrol to the same location.

When I arrived at the station, I was assigned to sit with the car in the garage. When the vehicle was searched, they found two revolvers and a mini 14 (a semi-automatic assault rifle), all fully loaded. One of the revolvers was actually the murder weapon. The deceased was not shot with the gun but he was beaten to death with it. A small part of the wood stock was found during the autopsy embedded in the victim's head. After the lawyers and the courts were done with all the motions we went to trial. I testified and the subject was sentenced to 25 years to life. Case closed!

Mental Health Cases

At one point I was starting to think I was in charge of people in need of mental help because I was always getting that type of call. For example, one night I had a call for a vehicle striking a home in Saratoga County. When I got to the scene the homeowner was the first one I spoke to. She advised me she was asleep in her room and she heard a large noise and the house shook. She said she went to the living room and there was a woman she did not know sitting on her couch. As soon as they had eye contact the woman on the couch said, "Quick get me two Kotex." She soon realized that the women had run into her house with a car and then entered through an unlocked door and sat on her couch.

After I interviewed the person, I believed she was in need of mental help, but she refused to go to a designated Mental Health facility. Instead, she wanted to find a judge and have her husband arrested for violating his marriage contract. I told her to get in the back of my car and lay down on the seat so her husband, who she claimed followed her everywhere, would not see her. I told her myself and another Trooper would drive her to the judge's office so she could get him arrested. We started south, heading to the Albany Medical Center hospital. It was the designated facility staffed to handle this type of case.

Each time she would raise up and try to look around, I would tell her to duck because her husband might spot her. When we arrived at the medical center and the car stopped, she realized what was going on. She jumped out of the car and started to run up the ramp. My young partner ran her down and brought her back. She was really pissed at me. She bitched and complained and then she spotted a phone booth and ran into it closing the door behind her. I knew that we were in for a wait because she had to see a head doctor and it would be awhile before they would have one available.

I told the Trooper with me to locate the doctor. I left her in the phone booth thinking what will it hurt? If she is there, I can keep my eye on her. After my patrol partner left to locate a doctor, I saw that she was dialing the phone and thinking it would occupy her. I did not try to intervene.

Suddenly, I heard a large squeal of brakes and four Albany uniform cops came running in the door with their nightsticks at port arms. I say, "What's going on guys"? The officer tells me their dispatcher got a call from a woman that some crazy man had her trapped in a phone booth! I told the Albany guys that it's fine, I do have her trapped and one of us is crazy, but it was not me.

They soon leave and my partner shows up with the shrink. The doctor is from the orient and I could hardly understand him. The woman we brought in is from Eastern Europe and has a heavy accent. I thought to myself what a country.

* * *

Another mental health case I had involved a check on the welfare of a person in a residence. I patrolled to the area, located the residence and everything looked all right. I got out of the car went onto the stoop and knocked on the door. There was no response. I knocked again. I look in the window and I see that everything that can be broken is broken. All the chairs, tables, TV and everything else is broken up in the house.

I called for backup when no one answered the door. As I looked around the house, I spotted the occupant of the residence peeking at me from behind a couch. I yelled, "Hey open the door. I want to talk to you". He responded, "Get off my fucking porch. I've been shot up bad in Nam and I don't put up with no bull shit". I asked him his outfit and he said that he was a Sergeant in the fighting 5th Marines. I told him I was a Corporal in the 4th Marines, and he came over and opened the door and let me in. I entered and saw a man about six foot two inches, hard as a rock and strong as a bull. I can see my backup

68

car arriving and soon the Trooper, Tom Sweeny, can be seen walking up toward the house. As I let him in, the Marine is aware of what is happening. We both grab my new friend Bill and he fights us, but we get him cuffed. I wanted to check the house before we left with him for further damage or victims. I stepped into the next room and I see, leaning against the wall, a high-powered rifle. I thought early on after I first saw him of just walking back to the car but I am glad I did not. Who knows what might have happened.

We explained to him were going to take him to the hospital. He told us he was an outpatient at the Veteran's Administration Hospital and he asked if we could take him there. I told him we would try. After we arrived at Veterans Hospital in Albany, we went inside and they gave us a room to wait for the doctor. When the doctor arrived, I took him aside to explain our case to him. The Doctor was a young man in his mid-20s and he advised us we would have to take him to the Albany Medical Center, as they were not equipped to handle mental health cases. I had left Trooper Sweeney with Bill still in handcuffs in the hall but he seemed to be OK. Bill looked into the area I was in with the doctor and the doctor said, "Sonny sit down!' The subject went a little wild and started moving towards the doctor exclaiming, "I've been wounded three times in combat, don't you call me Sonny you son of a bitch." We talked to him and brought him down. He finally settled down. I went back to talk to the doctor and he did not take his eye off the prisoner until we left to go to the Medical Center.

When we arrived at the Medical center, they were waiting for us and brought us into a room with a long table. We sat at the table with two orderlies and the head shrink. The prisoner and I at one end and at the far end the head doctor. We all sat down and the head doctor started to talk to the prisoner. After a few minutes, the doctor excused herself, said she would be right back and left the room. As soon as she left, the subject looked at me and said, "I can bullshit her, but I know I can't bullshit you!"

We turned the subject over to the hospital staff and left the area to return to work. About a year later I found myself in the same general area and I stopped in to visit the Veteran. He answered the door in good spirits and invited me in. A small dog came out of nowhere and bit my lower leg. He chastised the dog saying; "Get out of there, you're going to break your teeth!" I was wearing large leather boots and the dog bite did not go through. We talked some and then I left. I would have liked to have kept him as a friend, and if he wanted to hear Irish songs I could have sung all he wanted.

Chicken Willie

Another case I had involved a murder arrest on Rapp Road in the town of Guilderland. I was in that area when I met Officer Bruce Resnick of the Albany Police Department. He advised me that the Albany detective division was attempting to arrest a black male on Rapp Road in Albany when he ran out the back door of the house and was headed toward the adjacent town of Guilderland. I thanked him for the information and started to look for him. I located where the attempt to arrest him had occurred. The detective unit was parked in front of the house with the doors open and the engine running. I took it upon myself to remain with the parked vehicle and arranged to park behind it.

I was only at that location a few minutes when I observed a black male run from the woods to the highway and he turned to run up the road. I slid in behind him with the troop car and I do not even think the man knew I was behind him. He went up a steep hill and turned into a driveway that was also elevated. At the top of this driveway was a women sitting in a car with the motor running. At first I thought she was waiting for him but when I dismounted to grab him, I could see she was hollering at him to get away from her car. Once I got out of the car and grabbed him, he was struggling to get away.

71

I Jammed the muzzle of my pistol into his ribs and he still was moving around. When I got the cuffs on him the women told me she had no idea who he was or what he wanted. I was amazed at the way the man still struggled to get away even at gunpoint! I decided to turn him over to the Albany Police Department as the case they had on him was for felony rape. The patrolman came by again and I flagged him over. We both got out of our vehicles to switch handcuffs and while we are doing that he was still trying to get away.

They transported him to the station, ran his fingerprints and came up with a hit on him from the New Jersey State Police ten most wanted list. He was also known as (AKA); "Chicken Willie". He had killed a man in a bar fight with a large knife.

Marines

Another incident I had on patrol was during the time of the Vietnam War. I checked a pedestrian who was on a controlled access highway. The subject showed me some ID, but I also found a military ID on his person. When I file checked him it came back that he was not wanted. I then located his social security card and his number came back as a deserter from the United States Marine Corps. I had served in the Marine Corps for four years' active duty and I thought he needed arresting.

The man had shoulder length hair, was in need of a bath and many other things. I transported him to the State Police Loudonville Headquarters and notified the Marine Corps so they could get the military police in route to pick him up. After about an hour, I get a call to go to the front desk and see the Marine Military Police. For most of the hour, every Trooper in the building was busting my balls because of this fleabag looking deserter I brought in. When the two Marines arrived to pick the deserter up, the Marines looked like they had stepped out of a recruiting poster. Not a hair out of place, all leather shined and brass ready for inspection. I called a couple of the troopers over and said these guys are Marines, just in case you guys were wondering what a real Marine looked like.

Keough and Gavitt

One afternoon shift I was working with Trooper Bill Gavitt in the Guilderland area and noticed a large limo making a U-turn in an area where U-turns were not allowed. We stopped the vehicle, approached the operator and asked him about the U-turn. The operator and passenger seated in the front seat were Hispanic. They were both well dressed and the limo was fairly new. The operator stated that he had u-turned because the passenger in the back seat was ill and wanted to go home. I told him to open the side rear window and we might be able to help the passenger.

He activated the rear window switch and the window came down. The rear window was tinted very dark and until it came down I could not see inside the car. When the window opened, I could see a man holding a bag containing about three ounces of cocaine. I opened the door and tried to grab him but he went over the seat so I would not be able to reach him. I just stepped back from the door and sicked Gavitt on him. About a minute later Gavitt came out the door with the bad guy in one hand and the cocaine in the other. The bad guy had powder all over his face. While processing him, we found out he was an engineer who worked for the State of New York designing bridges. We turned him over to the BCI knowing they were going to make some good arrests out of the information he would give them.

On the same post, Bill Gavitt and I had one of the best criminal arrest of my career. We had a complaint assigned to us by Loudonville dispatch. The complaint was a domestic disturbance in the town of Guilderland involving a man and a woman. The dispatcher believed the man was armed with a knife. We patrolled to the area of the complaint and the woman answered the door and let us into her apartment. I asked her what happened to her husband. She advised us that he was in the room over there (pointing) and she said she thought he might be sleeping.

I walked up the hall to the bedroom she pointed out. I asked her what he and she were fighting about at this time of night. She stated that he would not stop going up the hall to the other bedrooms. I checked out the other rooms. The woman had eight children, seven of them were in one room and a fourteen-year-old girl occupied the remaining room by herself. I went into the young girl's room and she related to me that the man had been molesting her for a long time. I let my partner know what was going on and then I got in bed with the child molester, located his knife and arrested him. We transported him to the station and notified the BCI.

A few months later, I had to appear in family court in the county of Albany, and got to see some of the show involving this animal. While I was waiting to be called to give testimony, the woman who was the mother of the children, complained that social services pulled her allotment when they took the children away. It was also thought that the man had been molesting all the children and he was going to face additional charges.

When Bill Gavitt was riding alone in Guilderland, he had a radio call to check on the welfare of an older women who had not been seen in a while and people were concerned about her welfare. He entered her home through a window and found the old lady unconscious on the floor. He contacted medical personnel to respond to the scene to assist. After everything was settled, they found the women had fallen and broke her hip. When she got to the hospital they took her temperature and found it to be very low. The doctor contacted the barracks and asked them to send a patrol to the residence and check the thermostat to see what the setting was. Apparently, older people often turn the heat way down at night to save money. They also wanted to find out if she was taking any medicine.

I received the call because I was on the next shift. I gained entrance to the residence and found the heat was almost shut off. I then began to look for medicine. I had requested the lady who lived next door come with me and she came right over. The first dresser I looked in had forty-six thousand dollars in cash from her social security income. I immediately notified troop Headquarters and they sent a BCI man to assist in the inventory. I gave the hospital the information we had come up with but unfortunately the women died.

The neighbor told me she used to be concerned about the little old lady not having any decent clothing and she purchased some for her once in a while. I also found a purse sitting there and started going through it and I located some more money. I notified the BCI man that I had found more and the neighbor women who had been helping us said, "That's my purse!", so I returned it to its rightful owner.

Another night with Bill Gavitt at the Drummer Boy Bar on route 20, we spotted two young men on foot in the parking lot looking over the parked cars. As we start toward them Bill finds two other subjects hiding in a van truck and on the floor of the truck are three pieces of electronic equipment that have been torn out of someone's dashboard. There are still pieces of the dash attached to the equipment. After we processed the subjects and finished the case we stopped at the Rotterdam Police Department in an attempt to locate an owner of the equipment but it was negative. They advised us that there are quite a few stolen electronic devices in that town. At the bar, the subjects were located and we arrested them. They never entered the building and none of them were old enough to drink.

I had a business relationship with the owner. He always turned in people that were dealing drugs or using them in his business. He brought me into the restroom to show me the holes he had drilled in all of the flat surfaces to prevent people from snorting coke. He wanted his customers to enjoy themselves but any high should come from the alcohol, not drugs. I got along pretty good with him and information I had gotten from him was accurate.

Bill Gavitt is now a captain in "G" troop at the new State Police "G" Troop Headquarters in Latham, New York.

My Partner Baretta

I received a call to report to the Town of Altona in "B" Troop's patrol area for a missing person case. I drove quite a while to get there and I thought on the way up, why aren't they using their own K-9's. "B" Troop had a few bloodhounds assigned to them. I continued up and reached the area. A Sergeant from South Glens Falls was at the scene. He was the only other Trooper I saw in the area. He advised me to report to the forest ranger in charge of the search detail. I did so and the ranger gave me a few access roads he wanted me to check for fresh tracks.

I completed that check with my K-9 Barretta. When I was done, I went back to him and reported that there was no sign of fresh tracks on any of the roads I checked. I requested to be allowed to check the area the man was last seen in. The ranger advised that area had already been searched by people on foot. He also told me I could go ahead and check the area again and he gave me an

Environmental Conservation Officer (Encon) to take with me.

We went to the last area the man was seen in and entered the woods about thirty feet apart. As we were moving thru the brush the dog gave me an indication there was something off to my right (the Encon officer was off to my left). I yelled to the Encon guy to come over my way and he acknowledged me. After we went a little further, the dog wanted to go right again. I yelled to the Encon guy I was moving to the right. I spotted the old man moving through the trees ahead of me. I yelled for the Encon guy again and I got over to the old man. I believe he was eighty-three years old and I said to him, "I got you guy. We're going to get you out of the woods soon!" His answer to me was "I can't leave yet. I still have a lot of wood to chop!"

I gave him to the Encon guy to bring him out. I wanted to fire some signal shots and I didn't want the noise of the gun to scare him. I then headed to the road and soon after I hit the road the Sergeant pulled up and asked me if I had discharged my weapon. I told him, "yes" that the dog had found the guy. On the way back to my home station, I stopped at the nursing home there. They advised me that they had taken the residents for a walk and the old guy just slipped away from them. They were very happy to get him back.

One-day dispatch sends me through a radio call to a gas station on state route 7 in the Town of Niskayuna. Upon my arrival, the owner invited me in and showed me an artillery shell. It was approximately three-foot-long and about four inches in diameter. The fuse hole was empty. I brought the dog over and without hesitation he alerted indicating it was a live shell. I obtained a pad and made some notes about the shell. It had a brass band on it. The bands are common with large artillery as they make the projectile spin as it goes through the cannon barrel. It makes for a more accurate shot. It was evident to me that this piece had already been through a gun barrel because it has marks from the lands and grooves of the cannon barrel. The large steel casing also has marks indicating it bounced around on the ground.

I contact the U S Army 146 disposal unit at West Point on the phone and spoke to a sergeant. Based on the description I gave him, he advised me that we had a 155 Howitzer round and because the shell showed signs of being fired he said it was live and most likely suffered a fuse malfunction. He further advised me that it contains 12 lbs of TNT and the shell could destroy a city block. Members of the 146 disposal unit responded, placed the shell into the Explosive Ordnance Disposal unit and took it back to their army base for disposal.

Another case I had with an explosive occurred in Deer Park. Baretta and I were flown there on a helicopter. When I arrived at the scene I was briefed by a BCI member. An explosive was used to enter an ATM machine at a bank on the previous night. I was called to check on an item they located outside the bank by a power pole. One of the people at the scene thought it might have been a "gotcha" bomb. A "gotcha" bomb is something left behind to explode and injure investigators that had arrived at the scene to investigate the first explosion. I took the dog to the location and he checked the area without alerting. I told the bosses that I checked the area with negative results.

Sergeant Hornberger asked me to check the inside of the bank. I directed the dog in that direction. The dog alerted on a bottle on a desk in one of the bank offices. I advised Sergeant Hornberger and he took the bottle to be checked at the lab. The explosive that was placed in the ATM blew the machine out of the wall and left a hole big enough to drive a police car through. The floor was covered with broken concrete and concrete blocks. It was hard for me and the dog to walk around the premises. The bottle the dog alerted on was nitroglycerin.

When we were finished, we were transported back to the helicopter and departed for Albany. After about a half hour of flying, the pilot advised he was going to put the chopper down and he landed it in a train yard. After we landed he advised me a chip indicator on the dash of the machine lit up showing the transmission was having a problem. The light indicated metal chips were in the casing. Arrangements were made for me and my dog to be relayed back to Albany through troop cars. That meant It would be a while before I got home. The dog stunk from the rain and sat on the back seat from one car to the next. I thought the troopers were going to bitch about having the dog and me in their cars, but they were pretty good about it.

One night on a night call, I was advised Troopers from the Mayfield station received a burglary report from a neighbor who had spotted intruders in her next door neighbor's residence. She called the Troopers and when they got on the scene, they chased the two men out of the house and into the woods. It took me about an hour to get to the place and as I got out of the car, the Troopers at the scene told me that none of them had been in the wooded area. I soon discovered they were full of shit because there were tracks all over the area. I asked them who went in a particular direction and they blamed the sheriff's deputy at the scene. Two of the uniform Troopers went with me on the track, but everything had been run over, so I kept making circles and they would drop further back. I overheard them bitching about the dog not finding the suspects.

After about an hour of searching, I started to get an indication from the dog that he had a track. He started walking stiff legged and his hackles were up. It was pitch black out and I tried to keep my light out as much as possible. Soon the dog was pulling and I turned on my light and there was a man lying on the ground. I told him not to move or I would set the dog on him. He got up to run anyway. I discovered there were two men there, so I set the dog loose and when they started to run, the dog grabbed the closest one to him by the ass. The guy screamed like crazy and begged God to come down and save him from me and my dog.

At this point, the two Troopers that were following me came up and jumped into the melee. When one of the Trooper pulled the bad guy out of the dog's mouth, the dog went after the Trooper. After we talked to the suspects, we found that they did not know we had a dog with us. All of the police in the detail were acting like they just hit the lottery and I got to go home so the case went well.

At the Station in Loudonville at the end of our shift, Trooper Kevin Tuffey and I were doing our end of shift reports when the phone rang. It was the dispatcher at the other end of the building calling to say a man just entered the barracks holding a rifle and was looking for a Trooper by the name of Jim Foster. The dispatcher was John

Broderick. He was one of the best people we had. Although he worked as a dispatcher, he was more like a Trooper then most Troopers. John further advised me he asked the man if the gun was loaded and he replied that it was. I informed Tuffey what was going on and told him Baretta and I would go out the rear door and come back in the front and he should go up the hall and we would have the guy between us. The plan worked well. I stormed in the front door with the dog jumping up on his hind legs, barking and trying to eat the guy. It was a good thing I kept the dog leashed! I know we impressed the man because he pissed his pants. Normally, at the entrance to the building, there is an armed Trooper but at night he is required to make rounds of the building for security reasons so he was not there.

John Broderick was there to operate the radio and teletype system in the room next to the entrance. While all this was going on, there was a man sitting in the foyer where I captured the guy with the gun. We did not see him until we had the gunman in custody. After we had the bad guy cuffed, I yelled to the guy, "Are you with him?" and he said, "No, I just wanted to talk to someone about my driver's license."

One case with Baretta involved some young burglars in the Duanesburg patrol area and the Trooper involved with me was William Tyndale. The burglars had been caught but they had stolen a powerful handgun that had not been found. Two Troopers were sent into the woods to locate the firearm and they found everything else except the gun. Bill, Baretta and I went to the area in the woods to locate the gun. We found the area by the garbage they had left behind. I started the dog in a search and within five minutes, he located the gun.

I had a request from Investigator Robert Anslow about a case he was working with some stolen firearms that were hidden in the woods and had been there for a period of weeks. I followed him to the scene. When we got to the area, I let the dog go off the leash and within a few minutes he put his head down and when it came back up he had a rifle in his mouth. He dropped it and was looking for his reward. I said to Anslow "Did you see that because no one would believe it?" He acknowledged that he saw it.

At one time the Division of State Police sent me to a dog seminar at the Connecticut State Police Academy. I believe it was arranged by one of the G Troop Captains (God Bless them). They approved for me to bring Colonie Police Officer Bruce Harper with me because he was assigned a K9. We went in my Vehicle and when we got to the Academy we were met in the parking lot by a group of Troopers from Massachusetts and Connecticut. They were impressed by my dog. He was the first one they had seen from the Army. One of the Troopers asked me if we had any dogs that could detect guns I told them that my dog was the best New York had and that was the truth.

One of the troopers wanted me to demonstrate. I told him no problem but I wanted to use his gun so no one thought the dog was looking for my scent. He then took his gun and walked out into a field and hid the gun and returned to the parking lot. I then took the dog from the car talked to him for about five seconds and told him to find it. I had advised the Connecticut Trooper the dog will locate the gun and sit beside it looking at me for his reward, and that is exactly what he did! They were impressed and I went on to explain that the dog might have a harder time if the gun was thrown and the scent wouldn't lead up to it as in walking out and laying it down. We went in the academy to listen to the lectures by a Connecticut Trooper.

On our first break I went to my car to check on the dog and I found a crowd around it of Massachusetts and Connecticut Troopers. They requested I show them the dog locating another gun. I said sure put one out and he told me they already did. I get Baretta out and within five seconds, the dog has the gun located and in sitting next to it waiting for his treat. I gave him the ball and once again, I tell them it might be harder if you threw it his reply was "We did throw it!" I always was sure I had the best dog in New York and this just confirmed it. I never had that dog fail me when we were on a case. Not once. I know there were times when I should have paid more attention to Baretta and gone with his choice instead of mine but it was hard to understand that the dog was smarter than I was.

I had another caper with a G Troop Captain. George Abare called me into his office and told me to take my dog and get on Route 7 and enter Vermont and continue until I came to a Vermont State Police Road Block. He told me when I found it to stay with them as long as they wanted me. I entered Vermont and continued east for about thirty miles when I came on a Vermont Trooper by himself at a roadblock. I reported into him and he told me one of their Troopers had been shot by a burglar who had escaped. A large search detail was working up the road attempting to apprehend the desperado and he advised me his boss requested I remain at his position I advised no problem. After about a half hour they caught the bad guy and I went back to New York. The thing I noticed was the Trooper in Vermont was very young. I found out the age requirement was only eighteen years old to join the State Police in Vermont.

In another Dog case I was called to the city of Rensselaer at the scene of an armed robbery and shooting. It happened in a corner grocery store and the clerk was a fifteen-year-old girl who was shot at point blank range. Also at the scene was a teenage boy who was a customer and he was also shot. When I arrived at the scene, Pete Napic was the identification man present and he was doing a search of the scene.

I saddled up the dog and attempted to locate the perpetrator. The only track I had went from the store to a machine shop area less than a half mile away. I then returned to the crime scene to assist Investigator Napic with the search. One of the things he was looking for was the bullets that had entered the victim's bodies. We did not come up with any of the bullets and we got down on the floor and moved our hands around in the blood puddles trying to locate the bullets. We did not have rubber gloves at that time. Soon the hospital called and advised us they had located the projectiles in the bodies of the victims. The perpetrator was arrested and turned out to be an ex-convict. Both victims recovered and were able to describe what had happened and how they came to be shot.

One other airplane accident case I was involved in was with an Albany Police Lieutenant who owned a small aircraft that he kept at the Duanesburg Airport. He crashed it one day while practicing touch and go landings at the air strip. Something went wrong and the plane crashed and he was ejected from the airplane and was found at the scene deceased. The reason I became involved was because the Doctor that examined the body found what he thought was a pistol holster on the man's belt. There was no gun in it so they assumed it was lost on impact.

I reported to an agent at the accident scene from the Federal Aviation Authority and he guided me over the area the airplane had crashed in. He showed me a ditch the wing of the aircraft had dug in the ground and pulled some glass out of the ditch that was green in color. That indicated it was the port (Left) side of the aircraft as the starboard (Right) side should have red glass in it. At this time the dog is on his leash by my side but he is interested in something in the woods near us. I asked the fed if anyone else was with him he said no. I start over to the wooded area and find this guy wearing a large set of earphones and holding a large radio receiver in front of himself. I ask him what he is doing in this area and he shows me his radio and stated that it has picked up a signal from a downed aircraft. I bring him to the agent I am with, who reaches into the plane and pulls out something that looks like a small portable radio. He tells me this is the beacon that has been activated by the accident. I did not even know that small airplanes had such a thing. The guy retreats to wherever he came from to wait for the next airplane accident and I conduct a search for the missing gun.

89

The federal man tells me that if the man had something like a pistol on his belt it would almost certainly have come off in the accident. It started to get dark so I was calling it quits but I thought I would stop at the hospital to take a look at the holster the man was wearing because it might give me an idea on the case. I stopped and talked to a nurse and she was reluctant to let me view the holster but after considering it for a few minutes, she went and got it and brought it to me. As soon as I saw it, I was relieved because it was not a holster, it was a badge case. I contacted Zone and let them know what was happening with the case and went home.

On one of my dog cases, we received a call of a burglary in progress out of my station area but close to the borderline. We got to the residence and the house appeared to be empty, but the door was open. I harnessed the dog and entered the rear door with the dog on a leash. As soon as I got on the rear porch a cat that I had not seen, came out from under something made about three leaps and dove straight through the outside window which happened to be Plexiglas. I don't think the cat even knew a window was there. Baretta was not impressed with the cat's acrobatics. A short distance into the residence I located the burglar and arrested him. He was not from the area and was on foot. He was turned over to the BCI in Saratoga and I resumed patrol.

At one time, in the early days of the dogs I received a memo from Division HQ advising me that the two dogs in troop G had to be available for all local Police departments to be used in drug detection. It would be impossible to use a dog trained to detect explosives as a drug dog. No one was doing this in any department that I was aware of. If a dog gave an alert on a suitcase do you call the bomb squad or the narcotics unit? I contacted Captain Dan Kelly and explained the problem. Captain Kelly arranged to have a meeting with a full Colonel named Rasmussen. We all got together in the Captain's office in Loudonville. I was aware of Rasmussen and had talked to him before. He had always been a good man. I asked him how this detector dog was expected to work and explained the problem to him. He told me someone thought it was a good idea, but now he understood it would never work. The plan was abolished.

Baretta Searches for Prisoners on the Loose

Another type of call I would get was from the State Corrections Department relative to escaped prisoners. One of the first calls I had for a search was from Camp Summit in the southern part of Troop "G". Two inmates escaped in the area and when I got down there, the road was covered with new snow. Within a very short time I turned up a small side road with fields on each side of it. After I went about a quarter of a mile up the road, I spotted two fresh sets of tracks going up a hill in the fresh snow. I contacted one of the other cars on the detail and advised him of what I had located. I dismounted from the troop car, harnessed up the dog and started up the hill. I went about fifty feet and both subjects stood up to surrender. I stopped and held the dog while the other Troopers passed me to get the bad guys. This one was a piece of cake.

The next escape was in the daytime and everyone was there, the County Sheriff, State Police and Correction Officers. Everyone there wanted to be the one to put the capture on the bad guy. I was taken to the last place that the escaped prisoner was seen. I got ready to go and two Troopers came with me. We had a good track running through a field that was slightly overgrown, and I could see that the dog had started to lose interest, so I attempted to go back on the trail and ran into two Sheriff Deputies. Then I ran into three members of the Corrections Department. All of these people were interfering with any scent the inmate may have left. Now I knew why Baretta seemed to be not interested, but it was hard to explain that to them. After about an hour, we flushed the inmate from the wooded area and he was caught on the road.

The last track I ran at Camp Summit, the subject was not found and I begged to be released because I had just finished a night shift when they called me. The Sergeant approved my departure and I started back to my station. I only went a few miles and I saw and arrested the prisoner coming out of the woods on the side of the road.

The dog was always a big hit with the correction officers and they liked having us visit, the prisoners were not as thrilled. The prison had a large wooden ramp that went into the open yard of the camp. The ramp was enclosed with wood and a roof and when I came down the ramp with the dog the prisoners could hear me walking but they could not see us. When I reached the yard and stepped into the yard they would see the dog and start to run in all directions like it was the end of the world yelling, "Watch out here comes the dog!". Baretta never bothered any one at the camp though. Although I had other details to Camp Summit, none were as noteworthy as these.

One of my other dog cases comes to mind. I was called to Irish Hill Road in the Town of Berne to assist the Albany County Sheriff's Department with the case of a missing person who may have been depressed. When I arrived at the location I had a meeting with an NCO from the Sheriff's department. He advised me that they were trying to locate a resident of the county who had been reported missing and may be depressed. He requested I search the woods in the area as they had located the subject's vehicle. A deputy was assigned to go with me into the woods. I was then introduced to the deputy who was about six foot three inches and was armed with a twelve-gauge shotgun. We entered the woods and after a very short time the dog indicated he was on a good hot track. Suddenly he stopped and I looked down and the man's body was lying in a slight depression in the ground. A rifle was beside the body. It was a good case for the dog and was resolved very quickly.

Another case I had with my K-9 Baretta was with the Sheriff's Department in Schenectady County. I received a call from the Rotterdam Police Department about an armed robbery that had occurred in their town. I went to the scene and found that a dog from the Schenectady County Sheriff's department was at the scene with a handler by the name of Harry Buffardi. He would go on to be the Sheriff of Schenectady County. He is currently a college professor at Schenectady County Community College. In fact, my oldest grandson had him as a Professor for a criminal justice class.

We both attempted to locate the bad guy at the scene with negative results. After searching, we decided to secure the detail and advised the Rotterdam Police Department if they got anything else to let us know. I then went home and back to bed. Rotterdam called us back and said that the wanted person may have just ran out of St. Clare's Hospital in Schenectady. At the time I only lived about a quarter mile from the hospital, so the dog and I arrived very soon. Harry also responded. We talked briefly and went after the guy from two different directions. Shortly after starting the track, I could just make out Harry right in front of my dog and I think, what the hell is he doing over here. In a few minutes we are side by side and I start talking to him. Suddenly he yells, "Don't Move!" and I can just make out a man on the ground between us. I jump on the guy and we get him on his feet, but it turns out he was not the robber. He had entered the ER to request treatment having to do with some drugs he had taken. Harry and I both realized that the dogs knew where the man was, but we did not.

On one of the afternoon shifts I worked in Guilderland, I overheard a Guilderland Police Department unit receive a radio call about a stolen car in the town of Guilderland. Shortly after he put a teletype out on it, the vehicle was recovered by the town of Bethlehem on a road just outside of Guilderland. I patrolled into the area and located the vehicle. One of the Bethlehem members was still at the scene and I let him know I would attempt to track the bad guy from the vehicle.

I harnessed the dog and started looking for a track and within a few minutes I had the dog running on a good track into the woods. After a while, we crossed a muddy area and I spotted a footprint in the mud ahead of us. We kept going about a half a mile before we came to a farmhouse and the track went to the rear door. I walked around to the front of the house and noticed a road. Soon I saw a police car go by and I stopped it. I was aware that we might have a problem as we were in a strange property and the people in the residence may have been upset or have a dog that would become upset with us being in their yard. I wanted another Trooper with me when I knocked on the door and made my inquiry. The car I stopped was operated by Kevin Tuffey, a Trooper from my station. We both approached the door and a middle age gentleman invited us in.

I see a pair of wet boots on the floor with the same tread pattern I have been following through the yard. The man tells us his nephew had just come into the house and left his wet boots by the door. The name he gave us was a car thief from the town of Guilderland. The thief was interviewed and was lying to us. Even the uncle sees that! When we tell him we tracked him from the stolen car to the house, he is annoyed with us. When I ask him what he did with the keys to the stolen car he replies, "If that dog is so fucking smart, let him find the keys". Then we transported him to the Guilderland Station.

Once the city of Albany was having a series of armed robbery cases involving a sandwich shop. One night the manager, who was in possession of a registered handgun, fires at the bad guy and strikes him in the face. This caused a massive wound to his head area. They called me with the dog in order to locate the missing firearm from the bad guy. I started my track at the point where the shooting had occurred and we followed it until the track stopped. Along the way I came to a fence and there was a large amount of blood in the area. Then I realized why. The injured man had tried to climb the fence. He was found on the other side of the fence prior to my arrival at the scene. While he was climbing the blood was flowing for a longer period of time because he had stopped moving along and it was going straight down. Soon after this, a uniform officer searching the crime scene had located a toy gun believed to have been used by the perpetrator and I was released.

The dog was never affected by blood and gore. If anything he was attracted to it. The problem was he still wanted to play with the kids when he got home from work. In my house the wife was always a little afraid of the dog but the kids never were. They would bounce off the couch and land on the sleeping dog, who would just move to another spot. My wife learned to control the dog by ordering the kids to put him in the bedroom when she wanted to spank them. My three-year-old daughter, Colleen would grab the dog by his collar and lead him to the bedroom, and the dog went along without a problem. They eventually stopped putting the dog away for spankings.

Around the house he was like any other dog but with strange people knocking on the door or in his presence he was very protective of his family. One time I was in my cellar drilling a hole and my wife and children were on the first floor when a friend from work Jim Werthmuller stopped at my house in civilian clothing. My wife told him to wait a minute as the dog was in the house and she knew he might act. Jim told her it was alright because the dog knew him and he entered the house. Within a few seconds he was pinned to the wall and the dog was barking fiercely at him. I ran up the cellar stairs and subdued the dog and thanked him for his faithfulness. In that case the Baretta liked Jim and played with him while we were working, but the dog wasn't sure he had a pass to enter my residence.

Another time Jerry McGreevy and I had a car stopped and we were both outside the car talking to the motorist. The barracks called on the radio and as I was talking to the man, Jerry walked back to the car to answer the radio. Baretta was in the front seat with his eye on me and he was not moving. We switched positions and it was fine. I think most of the men I worked with liked having Baretta with us. Anytime the dog ran into children at work he was always a big hit.

Auburn Prison Riot

One of the other prison cases I responded to was around 1970 at Auburn Prison. They had a massive riot with the inmates taking over a large part of the prison and setting it on fire. I was working the day shift out of Loudonville when I was called in to the station through the radio. I could hear them calling other cars to return so I knew something was up. When I reached the station, Trooper Mike O'Brien was in the hall and he advised me we had to go up to the classroom. The Troop Commander (TC) was going to speak to us. When we got to the classroom on the second floor, the TC was already in the classroom with a Lieutenant from Zone 3 (Fonda). The TC advised us we were going to Auburn prison to assist in suppressing a riot. He told us we were not to drive fast on our way there and to be careful not getting hurt once we got there. He then turned us over to the Lieutenant. The Lieutenant told us we had a long trip to Auburn; that we would be taking the Thruway; and that our speed getting to our destination would be between eighty-five and ninety miles per hour. He emphasized the importance of us getting there forthwith.

I said to Mike, "Let's ride together to Auburn". He agreed and all we had to do was pick our car. We picked one that was the newest and in the best shape. We made sure it had fuel and oil and we got in line with the rest of the Troop "G" detail. After a couple of hours driving, we pulled up in front of the prison. It was fully involved in a large fire. Smoke was going up in the sky from a large building that was burning inside the walls. Upon our arrival, we were issued riot equipment consisting of helmets, shotguns and gas masks. Every other man assigned to the detail had a shotgun. Negotiators were talking to the prisoners trying to get them to give up, but it did not seem to be working. We were organized in ranks outside the prison in a parking lot at parade rest ready to go in.

As luck would have it, it started to rain. After we were soaked they opened the gates and we started in. As soon as we entered the inmates gave up. Our detail was stopped and we were brought back to the parking lot. After we formed up, we were advised to return to our respective troops. We drove back the same night. I believe this was before overtime was paid.

Whenever we worked overtime like this, the Sergeants would sometimes try to give us some comp time. For example, we would go to work on a raining day and the Sergeant might tell you to take a few hours off because of time they felt they owed you. I always wondered why they could not call you and tell you not to come in before you drove in to work!

Attica Prison Riots

During my next prison case in 1971, Mike O'Brien was once again my partner. We were both working the dayshift and they called us in again to return to the station. This time there was no screwing around. As soon as we came in the door, they told us, "Two men to each car, go to Attica Prison". "It's near Buffalo, get going". Mike and I ended up in the same car and we started to the prison. It looked like every member of the State Police was going to Attica. The Thruway was full of State Police vehicles heading west on I-90.

We did stop to eat, but none of us had very much money on us. When I left my house, my wife gave me enough for lunch and that was it. Fortunately, we stopped in at one of the rest areas on the way out and they allowed us to sign for our food. The trip to Attica was about 260 miles. When we arrived, the first radio transmission we heard from the Troopers that were already there was, "More body armor to the front". I am thinking, "What the hell? Are they shooting at us?" The only body armor the State Police had, had come in a case the size of a large foot locker. The armored shells we would put on (front & back) weighed about seventy pounds. Later I found out that the inmates had captured a 37 millimeter gas gun and they were shooting the gas projectiles at the Troopers in the hall of the prison. When they fired one, the Troopers on the front line would duck into an empty cell and the projectile would dispense the tear gas. However, because of the wind direction it would blow back at the inmates. When that gas dissipated, the Troopers tried to tease the inmate into shooting another round. It was my understanding, that the Troopers regained control of a wing of the prison by this method. Eventually one of the bosses made them stop.

Most of the first few hours were spent getting assigned positions. It was evident, the inmates did not want to play nice. As was normal for a detail like this, no one from the State of New York provided food for us. Obviously, we could not go in the prison mess hall because it was burning. This was only the first day. Our detail of "G" Troopers was initially assigned to an area right inside the wall on the lawn. We sat around in our assigned area until dark. Mike and I were then assigned to a detail with 10 other men. We were directed to get into ranks and they marched us further into the area the inmates controlled. During our march in, the formation of 12 had to keep stopping to unlock large gates made of chain link with razor wire on top. The gates were about

15-foot high. I thought when I looked up that I would not want to have to try to climb over these fences!

When we got to an area in the rear of the prison we stopped and were told this was our assigned position. They also told us they had lighting on the way. The correction officer who led us to this position also tells us if the inmates charge us, we would have to shoot them. Twelve men with eighteen pistol rounds each and we might have had twenty shotgun shells between us. I did the math in my mind. I did not feel well armed given that we were locked in with hundreds of rioting inmates.

The correction guards soon arrived with small portable spotlights that were gasoline powered. We set them up and got them working. We let him know that we were going to need more fuel and he said he would be back with it. He then left with the keys to all the gates we had just come through locking them as he went out. I realized we were trapped inside the prison with the inmates and the inmates started to act up.

One started out the gate towards us and a group followed him and they didn't look friendly at all. The Trooper standing next to me dropped down on one knee and racked the action of his shotgun. I know that sucker had a round chambered, so I said to him as calmly as I could given the circumstances, "Don't shoot him in the doorway." I was worried he may have fallen back inside. Shortly thereafter, I heard the safety on the shotgun click and I realize the shotgun is ready to go! I think every man on that detail heard the safety go off of that shotgun.

Mike O'Brien and I were ready to go back to back. The man leading the inmates started to climb up in the window bars then he just disappeared from our view. The other inmates did not come out of the building. We later learned the inmates that we thought were following the man as their leader, were actually trying to kill him. They did kill him as soon as he entered the building out of our sight. Our tour on the hill behind the prison continued and the generators started to run out of fuel. Soon both stalled. After they both ran out of fuel, the correction officer came back with fuel and gassed us up. After our tour of duty, we went back to the front of the prison by the same route we came in. The inmates that remained locked in their cells were cat calling at us and saying nasty things like "Who's sleeping with your wife?" and "We're going to kill you when you come back!"

When we first got to the prison our marching looked bad but the more they had us do, the better we looked. When we arrived back at the staging area all the good spots to sleep were taken. I found an old government issued trailer and I lifted the flap on the back and it was full of sleeping Troopers. One cot was empty and I knew

I had found my spot. Entering as gentle as possible so as to not wake everyone up, I soon got to the empty cot. I was just in time because it had started to rain outside and I was glad to be out of the rain. I laid down on the cot and soon realized why the spot was empty it was right under a leak in the canvas roof and the rain dripped down on my midsection. I said the hell with it and went to sleep.

The next morning the detail was getting bigger and bigger. More Troopers were arriving all the time as well as deputies from the larger sheriff's departments. The inmates were also getting visits from real wild lawyers. I imagine the lawyers could smell the money. The Black Panther Party sent people too. They were easily identifiable because most came wearing African garments consisting of long flowing robes. They all received a noisy welcome from the police officers. Soon we were told that if anyone cat calls at the visitors, they would be subject to discipline. The day that memo came out, I noticed a new group of sheriff deputies arrive and I stopped to say hello. Upon my arrival, the gate opened up and some panthers in robes came in. One of the new deputies let loose with a catcall. Apparently, they did not see the memo. Right in the middle of the group is one state police patch and I am wearing it. Talk about being in the wrong place at the wrong time! Late on the second day of the riot food arrived for us brought by the Salvation Army and it was free (God Bless them). We were all able to eat and the food was good. In the next few days the amount and different types of foods was staggering and we ate well.

One assignment there that sticks with me is a security detail I was assigned to at the point in the cell block where the police area ended and the riot area started. I was with a Correction Officer who was armed with a Thompson submachine gun. I was armed with a twelve-gauge shotgun and a .38 caliber revolver. After being on post for a while, an inmate calls and he is coming up to talk to us. The correction officer advised him to come forward. We both aimed our guns in his direction when he appeared. He mumbled something to the correction officer. I have no idea what he said at all. He might as well have been speaking a foreign language. I could not make out one word of what he said. I did hear the Corrections Officer tell him no. The inmate then left. I asked the Corrections Officer, "What the hell did he just say?", and "Why can't I understand him?" The Corrections Officer told me someone got stabbed and the inmates want a doctor to enter the cell block to treat him. The Corrections Officer told him that was not going to happen. They would have to bring the injured party up to us if he wanted to be treated by a doctor. The inmate left while bitching up a storm in a language I did not understand. Before long, the inmate returned with another prisoner carrying a wounded inmate.

There was much shouting between the inmates. The inmates set up a security system in the hall of the cell block. Their sentry would yell, "Who's there?" Someone would answer "It's me!" The sentry would say, "What do you want?" The other guy would say "I want to come through." He would answer "Go ahead." Then he would say "HALT!" It was always that kind of challenge. The prisoners wanted to appear to have a military operation but it was really insane. After a while, they got the injured inmate out to be treated by a doctor.

I was also assigned other jobs like to sit in cells that were empty and keep an eye on certain areas. At about the second day they had already killed one Correction Officer and wounded others. The state finally rented us rooms a short way from the prison and we were glad to have showers and clean clothes. This was a great feeling. They put us on two shifts day or night, twelve hours long. Although this sounds like long shifts, it was better than the shifts we had been working which were eighteen and twenty hour shifts. The only bad thing about the two 12 hour shifts was the sheets at the motel were not changed between shifts. One Trooper was exiting the room and another was entering it to sleep. At times, the guy leaving the room might leave you a can of beer, so it wasn't always bad.

I can remember going back to the motel one day and the pounding starts on the door meaning it is time to go back to work. I jump up get dressed go out in front and find that everyone else is up and they were already going back to the prison. I look at my watch and realize we have only been off duty four hours. The inmates had gathered up the hostages, who were all corrections officers and told the other Corrections Officers they were going to be setting them on fire. We were told we would be going into the block if that happened. Fortunately, that was a false alarm.

The bosses running this detail did not isolate the public from the prison. Relatives of the hostages were in front of the prison and most of them wanted us to take action sooner rather than later. They would yell out to us as we went by and our hearts went out to them as their loved ones were at the mercy of criminals many of whom had killed before. A large number of the correction department employees had relatives and friends working in the same place they were working in. In some ways, it was a large family, fathers, sons, brothers, uncles etc. As we drove by them, there was more and more yelling and it got louder and louder as the days passed. The inmates were parading their relatives around telling everyone they were going to set them on fire and cut their throats. They were holding large butcher knives to their neck while walking around the prison yard.

I had been calling my wife as often as I could. This was long before cell phones and sometimes she would be very upset and crying because the press was speculating on how many Troopers would be killed and injured when we took the prison back from the inmates. Then the day came when we were assigned to reclaim the prison.

We were all assigned details. Mike O'Brien and I got the power house detail. The power house supplies power to the prison. There was a Lieutenant in charge and we formed up in ranks in front of the power house. When the CO's and Troopers started taking the prison back, there was a lot of shooting. An army helicopter came overhead and dropped tear gas canisters creating a large cloud inside the walls of the prison. Before very long, we were brought into the prison to get the inmates back into their cells. I was walking up the cell block with Mike when we came upon a small Hispanic man lying on the floor. I ordered him to his feet and into a cell. He replied that he had suffered a gunshot wound and could not walk. The state police Sergeant on my detail is a great big man named Pushee. He can see me talking to the inmate, but he thinks the inmate is giving me a hard time and he yelled in a very loud voice, "Get into that cell!" The wounded inmate jumped to his feet and ran into the cell, gunshot and all.

Our next assignment was to search the prison for some of the missing inmates. We searched the prison laundry and boy did it stink in there. I thought we were going to find a body in that area. As I approached each dryer I would grab the handles turn my head and pull it open. The only thing we did find was some rotten eggs the inmates had put in the commercial dryers. These dryers were large enough to hold about three refrigerators each. Our search was negative for inmates.

Another assignment we had was escorting the inmates to buses that were transporting many of them to other prisons throughout New York State prison system.

After our work was done we were released to return to our troops. The press had a ball writing about the prison riot and the retaking of the prison. A positive thing that occurred on the way back was that people in the cars we were passing were clapping their hands and cheering us on a job well done. When we walked out of the prison after we retook it, I was very proud of the job we had done. Except for the loss of the Correction Officers, I thought we did a good job. Every man on the detail was very sorry about the people who were killed but we felt the inmates chose the way the day ended.

For years, the State Government held hearings and had all kinds of meetings and committees to study what went on at the prison. The courts ruled on everything that we had done and what could have been done different. We were told we should not have used our ammunition taking the prison back. But three years later the first Sergeant had me load all the emergency equipment including ammunition into the truck for another prison riot. It was the same ammunition we used at Attica. Fortunately, we never went to that one because it was all over before we arrived.

Comstock

The next prison job I was assigned was at Comstock prison in "G" troop. I was assigned to a detail during a strike by many of the Correction Officers at that prison. We were sent to back up the ones that remained working. My assignment was as a roving patrol inside the prison grounds. The "G" troop officer that was in charge of the prison detail loved the way the dogs worked on the gate assignments and in the prison itself. We had a few incidents.

In one case, a car with three members of a loud nasty motorcycle group tried to come through the gate to visit people. Every person entering was subject to search. We stopped the vehicle and started to search it and the occupants. We found a small handgun located in one of the coats in the back seat, but they all denied knowing who it belonged to, so we arrested all three. A group of Corrections Officers watching the search gave us a big cheer for that one. Most of the Corrections Officers got along with the Troopers pretty well. We both handled the same class of people. During the strike they would have fires burning and would be cooking over an open flame. They did much better than I would do with a full kitchen. We were often invited for dinner and the food was great.

While I was assigned the prison grounds detail, I had a call from radio dispatch to assist the State Police Whitehall patrol in the village with a complaint. The Trooper asking for assistance was one of the Paquet brothers. He advised me that a woman and her husband were in a local motel with five small children in the room. He had a warrant for the father charging numerous counts of burglary. The Family Court also requested the Trooper to take the children into custody. We went to the motel and knocked on the door. I could hear the mother telling the children, "The police are going to take you away from us so go and hide." I told the Trooper to hang on a minute and I would be right back.

In front of the building I had noticed a small gas station with a supermarket next door. I went into the gas station and borrowed a pair of bolt cutters from the owner. I then went to the supermarket and bought a large bag of peanut butter cups and I went back to the motel. Nothing changed at that location in my absence. The witch is still talking to the kids about the bad police and scaring the hell out of them. I open the door with a passkey and reached in with the bolt cutters and cut the chain. The kids were all trying to hide in the closet. I paid no attention to them and I just went over to the bed and sat on it and started to eat the peanut butter cups. Within a couple of seconds, the kids joined me on the bed eager to have a piece of candy. The mother was handcuffed and put in the back of the police car where she belonged. Using the bolt cutter on the door was done for two reasons. One, to keep the door from being broken more than necessary and two, it would have scared the kids if we crashed through the door.

That night I was able to get into the Village of Whitehall, so I let the men in the towers at the prison and the other posts know if they wanted anything to let me know and I could pick it up for them. My first order came from Trooper Dave Foster. He asked me to go to a good cigar store and pick him up some cigar I had never heard of before. I said, "Dave you are in Whitehall, NY, no cigar stores could survive in this area".

I had another contact with Dave at his post in a prison tower. Trooper Bob Stampfli, a State Police rifleman had stopped at Dave's tower with his issued sniper rifle. Dave was watching the convicts lift weights at the other end of the yard. Bob's rifle was on a hook in the tower. Dave picked the rifle up, lifted it, and looked through the scope at the weight lifters. Everyone in the yard stopped what they were doing and froze in place thinking Dave was going to fire the rifle at one of them at any minute.

I got out of that tower and went to the next one that was manned by Trooper Tom Hudson. A few years later Tom transferred to the State Police Station in Saratoga. One night he was working the afternoon shift, 3 PM to 11 PM, and at the last half hour of his shift he returned to the station to fuel the car and do his end of shift reports. The desk man told him he was getting calls about a tractor trailer disabled on the interstate highway (I-87) at the Saratoga exit. Tom went out to check on it and the trucker got in the front seat of the troop car to call for a tow just before another tractor trailer came down the road and struck the troop car from the rear. He ran up on top of the troop car, setting it on fire, killing Tom and the truck driver. The vehicle had a fresh tank of high test gas. At Tom's wake, his wife went out of her way to come over to me and speak about Tom. We both loved him.

Back at the prison, I was still assigned roving patrol and I noticed a very large amount of small pink colored balls in the field surrounding the prison. These balls are what the inmates use to play handball inside the wall and when they are hit over the wall they cannot get them back until someone throws them back over the wall. I became like Santa. I obtained a large bucket and filled it with balls with Baretta's help. He thought he was in dog heaven because there were so many balls to chase. We returned them to the inmates by dropping off some at each tower. When the inmates saw the Troopers had the balls, they would click like a dolphin looking for a treat and the Trooper would throw them the balls. While we were on the prison strike detail the officer in charge kept the dog men on duty with no days off until the strike was complete. I thought it was great and they paid us overtime when we worked it. When I started on the job there was no such thing as overtime so I liked working it and getting paid.

High Speed Chase

Back on patrol in the Town of Guilderland I heard of a high speed chase coming my way from the west involving an armed robbery case that had occurred in the Duanesburg area. I start going west on route 20 in an attempt to get involved in the chase. The radio traffic picked up and soon the speed of the chase is given out as one hundred miles per hour, so I expect that my involvement will happen soon. Trooper Bill Khachadourian is calling me for a description of the vehicle being pursued. I have no idea what it looks like, so I tell him "It's the one in front of the police cars with their lights on!"

At this time, I hear the voice of Trooper Werner Hoffman, an old Duanesburg veteran Trooper on the air. He directs me to make my next left because the bad guys bailed from their vehicle and are running in the woods. Trooper Hoffman was not working and he had gotten a ride home from another Trooper in a marked car. When the chase started. He was operating the radio during the chase. When they bailed out, one of the suspects was apprehended at the scene. The other two fled up a snow covered hill. Trooper Hoffman directed me to the area they ran into. I ended up arresting the two that had fled the scene. I spotted them in the woods trying to hide. They were less than fifty feet away, an easy shot for a pistol. When they saw I had my sights in on their heads, they gave up. As soon as I got close enough, I put the first one down in the snow without taking my gunsight off the second one. I was aided by investigator O.J. Hughes from State Police Duanesburg and he put the second one down. A few months later, we all were invited to a city in the southern part of the state and each member that was involved in the capture of the three received a ribbon from a support your police group.

A funny thing that happened after the bad guys were arrested was that as I walked back up the hill to my unit, a Guilderland PD unit was parked next to mine. Sergeant Gary Lee, a police paramedic said to me, "Don't worry Jim, I've got the heart machine all warmed up in case you need it." He was always a great ball buster. Trooper Dan Davidson initiated the chase, so naturally I had to bust his balls about being the last one at the scene of the capture.

Serial Killers

In my time as a Trooper I was assigned a number of search details. One involved the search for Robert Garrow up in the Adirondack mountains. Garrow was wanted for killing a camper. I did not have a dog then, but I ended up on all the searches for Garrow starting with the first detail in the Wells, New York area. I received a phone call at 4 AM one morning and I was ordered to report to work for a manhunt that was being conducted in relation to a recent homicide. I got dressed and reported to Troop Headquarters in Loudonville, New York. When I arrived, I was sent to the Wells area with one other Trooper.

We drove up to the scene and were advised that three young people were camping in a wooded area near Wells when they were approached by a man armed with a rifle. He took all three into his control. He tied the male

117

and female to trees with their hands behind them, and he took the third male into the woods by himself. The kids were scared but they had not seen anything yet. After a very short time they heard their friend struggle with the man as he started to choke and stab the kid. The male and female who were tied up, broke free of their ties and ran like crazy to get away from this man. They somehow got to a phone and that is how the State Police got involved.

After I arrived at the scene, I spent the first night guarding a logging road in the area. During the night, I talked to two Troopers who had stopped their cruiser and got out to take a leak. They spotted a car moving on the logging road without lights, chased it until the operator lost control and ran off the road. The operator took his rifle and fled the scene and they could not locate him in the woods. This led us to believe the bad guy was still in the area, so roadblocks were set up to contain the suspect.

I had all types of assignments on this detail... some were not so good. One day they dropped me off at the end of a logging road and left me there for a few hours. A captain came up to check on me and he said, "Jim how are we going to know if you see him if you don't have a radio?" I replied, "Captain, you don't have to worry about me, I have a twelve-gauge shotgun, you'll be able to hear that!" He stopped in his tracks and started to explain to me that the man might have committed other crimes, so they wanted him alive if possible. It turned out the man was a serial killer and he wanted the girl in this case which is why he started to kill the males first. They left me on that post with nothing to eat or drink for nearly the whole day. Finally, a BCI guy I knew came through for me in the afternoon. He brought me two slices of bread with mayonnaise on them, no meat and a couple of drinks in cans. We stayed on that detail for about a week until Garrow escaped the Wells area by stealing a car. The Trooper that was in pursuit had a severe problem with his vehicle and had to stop the chase.

The entire detail was moved further north up to "B" troop because that is where Garrow was headed. A few days later Garrow suffered a gunshot wound when running from the police. An Environmental Conservation Officer (ENCON) hit him with a pellet of buckshot in the lower leg and he milked that wound in prison. After he was wounded, he claimed all kinds of pain and problems. While in prison, he refused to walk at times or work because of his gunshot wound. However, he was able to scale the fourteen-foot fence with his bad leg when one of his relatives smuggled a gun to him in prison and he used it to escape. During this escape he also shot and wounded a Correction Officer with that gun that had been smuggled to him. He was eventually shot to death by a

119

Correction Officer during his escape.

At another time in another serial killer case I was assigned to work on a homicide in the city of Schenectady. Two other Troopers were also assigned with me Trooper Dave Foster and Trooper James Foster. We reported each day to the Schenectady police department and they would assign us details. At times we would conduct interviews and searches. One of the interviews we did was at an adult store and when you entered the place you had to walk around dildos that were so big they had feet. All six foot three inches of Dave Foster asked the owner if he has had any one strange in the place. I told Dave anyone that went into that store had to be strange. When the detail was secured we all went back to our post and continued our patrols.

The killer in this case was a serial killer who would visit our patrol area again. His name was Lemuel Smith and he would kill some more before he was put away. He killed a young woman in the Colonie Center parking lot in her vehicle while the mall was open and running. He also killed two people in the city of Albany.

Smith was caught when he went into an attorney's office in the city of Schenectady, kidnapped a girl working there at gunpoint and brought her to a residence in Saratoga County. He kept her at that location and raped her over and over again. Then he got in her car with her and had her drive him to the town of Colonie. He first gave her a bath and insured that she washed properly to destroy any evidence.

Her parents attempted to report her missing but the police department would not send a teletype message until she was missing over twenty-four hours. The parents went to a friend who was an officer on another Department and he put the girl on the teletype. The girl was sighted driving erratically and stopped by the Colonie Police department. The officer noticed that the operator was very upset and invited her to come back to the police car with him. As soon as she got out of the car she yelled, "HE HAS A GUN", and the officer took him into custody. It had to be the best arrest he ever made. The day after this incident occurred I took my dog up into Saratoga County and we found the pocketbook and preserved it for prints, but I do not remember if they found any prints on it. The defendant in this case went on to kill a female prison guard.

Lake Placid Shooting

Another search detail I was assigned to near Lake Placid, NY involved the shooting of a State Police Zone Sergeant in the Village of Lake Placid. It was another night call. We were called in to assist in the search for the man who shot Paul Richter, a Zone Sergeant assigned to "B" troop in Malone New York.

The Lake Placid patrol with two Troopers in the car was investigating a burglary that occurred in that area. The place that was broken into sold firearms among other things. The patrol located the car they were looking for connected to the burglary. It was in the parking lot of a bar that was still open. They notified the Zone Sergeant who was riding alone (as is normal). Paul got together with the Troopers and advised them to exit the village and stand by at the town/village line. The two Troopers backed off as the Zone Sergeant ordered. The Zone Sergeant contacted the village police department and they sent a one-man car from the village to his location.

When they saw the two subjects come out of the bar, they approached the two men who pull weapons and shot both the Sergeant and the Village Policeman. The village Police Officer returned fire and struck one of the bad guys in the shoulder, but they got in the car and take off. Zone Sergeant Richter took a round which severed his spinal cord. He was unable to move. The patrolman was able to notify the two-man troop car with the radio and they were soon chasing the bad guys. They fired their weapons at the fleeing vehicle and this goes on until they run into the next "B" troop car whose occupants set up a roadblock stopping the subjects. One of the subjects is captured at the stop location and the other one ran into the woods.

At that point, "B" troop reached out to "G" troop for additional manpower to search for the subject. When we got to the scene everyone was searching the area where the car was stopped. The bloodhounds soon arrived and they put about five men behind each bloodhound and they start up a very high mountain in the area. I was assigned with one of the teams. We went on and on chasing that damn dog. When we got to the top, the dog handler is telling the Lieutenant in charge about how tired his dog is. So they sent us down the same hill to switch out dogs. That new dog started from the beginning and up the hill we went again; new dogs but the same guys. This went on for a few days.

The guy was finally caught near his home. We went on twelve hour shifts for many of these cases and we were billeted in motel rooms at the end of our shifts. Most of us would do this type of detail for nothing because a fellow trooper needed us. When this guy was apprehended near his home, we were all sent back to our troop's to return to normal duty.

D Troop Shooting

Troopers from "G" troop were involved in another assist involving a trooper who was shot while working out of the State Police Pulaski station in "D" Troop. He stopped a vehicle with two men in it, on a back road and the operator told him his license was not with him. He said he left it in a residence just down the road where he was staying. The Trooper spotted a rifle in the car, but it was in a case and he gave the operator the benefit of a doubt and told him he would follow him to the house so he could display his license and registration. He started to follow the guy on the back road, but unbeknownst to him the passenger loaded the rifle.

The operator pulled over again as did the Trooper whereupon the trooper saw the muzzle of the rifle come up over the seat. He put the cruiser in reverse and gave it the gas, but he was not quite quick enough. The passenger fired striking the trooper in the head with two rounds killing him instantly. The troop car still in reverse continued off the road. The two desperados left the area quickly. It also was a little while before they found the deceased Trooper. I understood at the time that it was his brother who found him who was also a Trooper stationed at the same station.

I was notified to return to Loudonville as per the troop commander. Once again within a very short time I'm on my way to an area close to the scene of the shooting. Milt Rembach was my First Sergeant at the time. He was one of the best First Sergeants that "G" troop had and when his kids were small, I played Santa for them. His one son became my Zone Sergeant years later. Milt Rembach assigned me to a unit with a Trooper that did not talk to new guys. Trooper Jim Corbett was stationed at State Police Selkirk. For the first two hours, all he would do was grunt at me and I was supposed to know what that meant.

We stopped every car that went by us and checked the people out that were in them. One of the things that I remember about that night was how cold it was. The local people that we were stopping were great and they brought us about five dinners apiece and coffee pots galore. They took great care of us and before the night was over Corbit and I were good friends.

The bad guys were finally arrested. I saw Corbit years later and I had heard that he and his wife had split up and she ran off with another retired Trooper. I asked him about it and he said, "Jim I really didn't care that she ran off with him. He was a good friend, but he took my best golf clubs when he left and that really bothered me."

Keough and Schreiner

Jack Schreiner was a trooper for quite a while with me. He also worked in the Guilderland patrol area. The best story Jack ever told me was when he was a City of Albany patrolmen and he took the State Police exam and passed it. When he was through with his interview and received a date to report into the State Police academy, he advised his captain that he was going to switch to the State Police and gave him his two week notice that he was leaving. The captain replied, "I don't need two weeks' notice, turn your stuff in today, you're done!"

Jack and I got along great. We worked together for quite a few years. One of the cases we worked on was a school burglary in Guilderland. It was his case, but he invited me to ride with him. I got in his vehicle with him and we patrolled to the scene of the burglary. Entry was gained to the Guilderland school through a loading dock area door. One of the things taken from the school was a large safe. As we were checking that area we noticed something at the far side of the parking lot on the ground. It turned out to be a registration plate for a vehicle. There was a dip in the ground and marks on the ground in the area where we found the plate. Evidently, a vehicle had dragged bottom and possibly lost its registration plate.

126

We received information from the Department of Motor Vehicle (DMV) as to the owner of the vehicle and went to the address of the registered owner.

The owner was glad to help and showed us where the vehicle involved was parked. As we approached the parked vehicle we observed the rear plate was missing. The owner gave his permission for us to look in the trunk of the parked vehicle. He unlocked and opened the trunk and we see two large pry bars and a sledge hammer. Everything was covered with cement dust (most older safes had a layer of cement inside the steel outer surface). The owner of the vehicle appeared shocked at what we found and he told us his teenage son was the last driver of the car. When we locate the kid, he gave us the location of the safe and property involved in the theft. The kid was prosecuted.

In another case with Jack Schreiner, we were working nights out of Guilderland and we got a call to patrol to a bar on State route 155 in the Town of Colonie due to a disturbance. There was a young man there they are holding as we arrive and we start to learn what happened. The young man had gone into the men's room to use the toilet and he noticed that the men's room and women's room shared a common wall. The man was very intoxicated and decided to climb to the top of the wall and look into the girl's room. He was able to get on the wall and in the process of looking over at the girls, one of them sees him and screams. In his attempt to get down, he slips and falls down through the ceiling knocking most of the ceiling tiles out on the way down. He also sustained injuries. When we take the boy into custody, both of us are concerned about what his parents are going to think. We did not want them to think we had anything to do with his injuries. It turned out we had no problem with the boy's parents. We charged him and released him to his parents.

A few years later, Jack called me to assist him again. We went to a motel on Central Avenue in the Town of Colonie on a suspicious person complaint. Upon arrival, he located a vehicle with a large safe in the trunk. As Jack knocked on the motel door, the bad guys went out the rear window and ran to a nearby junkyard. After a brief search we located both burglars and captured them. When Jack retired, I was sorry to see him go, but he got a better job taking care of his grandchildren.

DWI Arrests

This is the funniest DWI arrest that I was ever involved with and I had hundreds of them. I spot the guy going north on route 9 in the Town of Colonie and his car is all over the road. I turned my overhead lights on and signaled him to stop which he does fine. As I approached his vehicle, the operator says, "What's going on chief?" I answered, "You have the wrong guy. The Chief is the guy with all the feathers. I am a Trooper. Can I look at your license and registration?" He produced both and after some discussion with other people in the vehicle, I located a sober adult who agrees to drive the car away.

I took the drunk driver into my cruiser and started to the Loudonville station. We get there without incident and at that time we had to have a different member conduct the breath test other than the arresting officer. So I contacted Ray Van Buskirk who was cleared to use the machine and happened to be in the building. The test machine we were using at that time was the breathalyzer 900. Ray set the machine up and had the defendant sit in front of the machine. He took his time and gave him an explanation of how he was going to take this test.

When the time came, he handed him the hose to blow into the breathalyzer. The guy put the hose in his mouth, bends over and makes all kinds of blowing noises as his face turned beet red. Ray tells the guy you're not blowing hard enough. The guy takes the hose out of his mouth and says "I'm blowing as hard as I can." Ray replied, "No you're not! The machine did not get any air. Try it again". After two more attempts with no results, the guy says, "I'm not blowing into that machine again!"

A sergeant who was in the next room stepped in and said, "We have had women in here who could blow hard enough to make the machine work!" The drunk replied, "They must have done a hell of a blow job because I blew my balls off and it didn't work!" At that point, the defendant's brother enters the room and said, "Come on Joe, blow into the machine." Joe replied, "John, if I blew on your cock like I blew on that machine, I could blow you a fucking ulcer!"

During the conversation, one of the troopers looks at the machine and can see the dial is not in place to accept a breath sample. When he moved the dial, the machine was able to work. No matter what we told Joe though, he said he would not blow into the machine again. I tell him I am going to have to take him to the hospital for a blood test. He started whining that he will die if they put a needle in him. I get him to the ER, but he keeps yelling about how he will die if he has to take a blood test. I handle him as a refusal and the DMV did revoke his license after a hearing. I thought they would give him the benefit of a doubt but in this case they ruled in the state's favor.

* * *

One of the cases I had with a DWI that annoyed me was in the area of the Mayfield Substation at a DWI road check. I was assigned by my Zone Headquarters to assist at this road check in another zone. At the site we had a group of Troopers stopping vehicles and checking for DWIs. I was assigned by a Zone Sergeant to assist a local Mayfield Trooper with an arrest by going to the station and running the test on a subject for him. I did as ordered, but I did not see what the grounds were for the arrest. When I ran the test, it was negative for alcohol consumption. The man had no smell of alcohol or anything else that made me think he was drunk. I think the reason we tested him was he was in possession of enough marijuana for about one half of a smoke. There was no smell of grass in the vehicle. When we returned to the site, I requested the Zone Sergeant assign someone else to help this guy if he needed it.

* * *

On another occasion, Trooper Willard Schultz and I were on the Thruway in separate troop cars going back to our station from a DWI road check. We did not score any drunks, which was generally a usual occurrence. As we are heading back, I see in front of me a classic drunk. His car is all over the road and he is going about twenty miles under the speed limit. Schultz is not in sight, so I call him on the car to car channel and advise him of what I have and my location so he can join me. I then stop the defendant and he is about as drunk as a man can get. Schultz is now at the scene and he calls the thruway Troopers to handle the case. I would never have called the troopers from the thruway to handle anything but Schultz felt we should.

A few minutes later the Thruway assigned Trooper gets to the scene and he is bitching us up and down about bothering him with this drunk. Later I found that he was one of the drug interdiction Troopers and he did not want to miss the drug traffic for a mere DWI arrest. At the time, most of the drugs that the State Police confiscated came from thruway stops. He took the subject into custody and we returned to our station. The Trooper from thruway was so annoyed with us, but we were just doing our job but I am sure he thought we were keeping him from the drug arrest he was looking for.

* * *

We had a new person in our station and one night as we were on patrol we receive a radio message from our dispatch to interview a subject in the city of Schenectady about his car being stolen. The guy was in our patrol area earlier that night. My young partner grabs the mike and advised dispatch to turn the complaint over to the day shifts. I tell him no it is our case and we have nothing going on now. Dispatch is advised to disregard, that we will handle it. We go to the address given and locate the caller at a party and he is as drunk as a man can get. We tell him in order to handle the case we have to go to where the event took place. We drive to Frenches Hollow and low and behold we come upon his car rolled over on the side of the road. We call him a tow truck and after a brief interview we arrest him for driving while intoxicated, falsely reporting an incident, and leaving the scene of an accident. Now the day shift starts with a clean slate and we have some good activity for our night and it keeps the mean old zone Sergeants happy.

Women Join the Job

When the Division of State Police (DSP) started to hire females, I was assigned to the station they were all initially assigned to; SP Loudonville, Troop G Headquarters. I got along with them all and liked the idea of having females working with us. To this day I count Maureen Tuffey (Moe) as a close personal friend and when the old timers get together we both attend. Moe was the longest serving Trooper in the division when she retired in 2012.

* * *

In the 1980's, I was assigned to the substation at Guilderland and we had another young lady assigned to our station or at least she rode in our patrol area at times. Her name was Pat Grover and on one A-line shift 11PM to 700 AM, she was assigned as my partner. At the end of our shift, we would split up and she would drive back to Loudonville to turn in her car and sign out in the blotter. I remained in Guilderland to do the same thing. After she left the station and had gotten to the Town of Colonie I heard her on the radio that she was checking a person. She was advised by the Communications Specialist that the person was wanted and it was for some sort of sex crime. I went out, got back in the car and went to back her up. It turned out the section of the penal law he was wanted for had been entered improperly by the department that was the authority on the warrant.

* * *

Pat was transferred to the Thruway and worked out there for a few years and suddenly she appears at the Guilderland station one night and she has an arrest warrant for a woman in my patrol area. The defendant was a former customer of mine and the warrant is for driving while intoxicated. She wanted to go get her by herself, but I tell her, that's not a good idea as the women is a whore and she entertains at her residence and may have customers present when she arrives. I ask her to give me a few minutes and I will go with her to assist. We drive to the residence on a back road and as we turn in the driveway, we see the house was dark. We approached the home and there is not a sound. Pat knocked on the door and we still did not hear a sound. I reach over her and pound on the door and yell, "Nora open the door goddamn it!" Nora replied, "Jim is that you?" I said, "Yes! Now open the door!" The door swung open and there stood Nora in all her glory half dressed, picking at her hair. I said, "Nora, is that the way you treat me?" She replied, "Jim, I'm sorry, I didn't know it was you!"

At one time when we were at Nora's house on a

135

complaint, there was a man in her bedroom with a handgun so I wanted to be sure the residence was clear. I told Nora I was going to check the back room (her bedroom). I went back to the bedroom, but the man there checked out OK. After I got back to Nora, Pat told her we had a warrant for her and she was going to go for a ride. After a little jerking around, we got her into the back seat of the troop car and we headed to my station so I could pick up my car. All the way back Nora, was telling me all her problems and explained to me that she was in some guy's car coming home from NYC on the Thruway and the man was driving over 100 miles per hour. She said he passed a Trooper writing a ticket on the side of the road so he pulled over to the right and shoved her behind the wheel and off they went. The Trooper saw them change places and when he caught them, he arrested both for DWI.

Pat Grover went on to become the field commander of the New York State Police. Good for her and God Bless her, she worked hard for it and she deserved it.

Crossgate's Mall

One of the things that we had going for us in Guilderland was on a day when there was nothing going on we always had Crossgate's Mall to fall back on to keep busy. It was always a good spot to look for a crime to occur and I had a lot of good arrests in the mall. I used to make a concentrated effort to keep an eye on the parked vehicles and this led to some good arrests.

During one trip through the parking lot in daylight, I spotted two young men sitting in a car in the middle of the lot. As I got closer, one of the men took off a pair of heavy duty goggles. I stopped the car so I could talk to the occupants. When I approached the vehicle, I saw glass on the floor with a large hammer. Before I started talking to the passenger, I reached in the car with my large metal flashlight and taped the operator on the leg and told him to hand me the keys for the car. Once I had the keys I pulled the passenger out of the window and held him between the cars. I looked around and located a vehicle close to them with a smashed sunroof that they had just entered. It was a good "on patrol" arrest and the man who owned the damaged car was pleased.

* * *

I had a pair of field glasses or binoculars that I

carried on patrol and sometimes I would park in an elevated parking lot and scan the other lots. One night while I was doing this I saw a car stop in the lot. The subject got out and approached a parked vehicle. I saw something that looked like rain around the car he had approached.

He quickly ran back to the vehicle he had entered the lot in. I drove toward the car he was near in the lot and as I got close, I saw the ground was covered with glass. I changed my direction and located the subject in his getaway car and stopped him finding the stolen electronic unit he stole from the parked vehicle. While I was talking to him, the owner of the vehicle he broke into came over to report the theft. I had an open and shut case. That night the defendant's mother called me to tell me I had the wrong person. I explained to her what had occurred but she still insisted he had nothing to do with it. Her little innocent boy even had a device used by welders that is also used to break windows, but mom said he always carried one of them.

* * *

Other times in the mall, Trooper Willard Schultz and I, who normally worked the afternoon shift, would make a deal. I would handle most of the minor complaints we got in the town and he would work the mall complaints.

138

When one of us would get an arrest, both of us would work on it and get credit for the activity.

One of my better complaints in the mall came from a mall store that called the station to report a credit card being used in their store four times in thirty minutes. I got to the store as soon as possible. While I was talking to the salesman, the manager told me he just looked up the walkway in the mall and the man and the women who had the credit cards were on their way back to his store. I told him to go in front of the store and let me know when they arrive. He left and soon let me know when they were back. I stepped out and grabbed the male. He was not a problem at all, but the woman was walking around me in circles calling me a "Motherfucker", and screaming at me. I told her that she spoke very strange for a doctor. Soon an off duty town police officer came by and I asked him to drag her over to me so I could get a set of cuffs on her and he did. The reason I was telling her she had a strange vocabulary for a doctor was because the credit card was made out to an MD. I later found out she was arrested for something else in Albany Co and was sent for a psych exam. While the doctor was out of the examining room for a minute, she stole her wallet and was blitzing the mall with her man.

* * *

One time when I was on my way back to the mall to release a subject I had arrested and processed at the station, one of the security guys from the mall grabbed me and told me they had a fight going on in a shoe store in the mall. The security guard takes me to the shoe store. The scene was unbelievable. Every display they had was tipped over and shoes were everywhere. It was hard to walk up the aisles. Two large women were still engaged in hand to hand combat in the store and about thirty to forty people stopped shopping to watch the fight. I soon learn that one of the women is employed at the store the other is a shopper. They lived in the same neighborhood and did not get along.

I attempted to stop the fight and the shopper hauls off and aims a kick at my wiener. Directly after the first kick, she delivered another. I spun back and forth to avoid the kicks and delivered a leg sweep that put her on her ass with me on top. I get her face down and as I was ready to handcuff her, I reached around her to get her other arm and she turned into a gator. She bit me on my forearm drawing blood. All the while, we are rolling around on the floor, her husband is standing there watching us. He is about six foot three inches. After she finally gives up, she asked me to let her up. She said she was going to forgive me. All I want to do is lock her up. She finally calmed down some and I was able to get her on her feet with her hands cuffed behind her back. The husband then intervened and said he wanted to straighten this thing out without her being arrested. I told him no way and called for another car. When we got a second Trooper at the scene we transport her to the station and process her as we do all arrestees. She pled to a reduced charge and was sentenced to thirty days in the county jail. I had to go to the hospital and get a tetanus shot!

* * *

On another occasion, I happened to be driving through the mall lot. The mall was very crowded and the people are in one large mass. As I looked closer at them, the mass of humanity started to part just like the Red Sea. I could see in the center were three large black male teenagers. The middle one was bleeding like no tomorrow. His entire upper body is covered with blood and the man looked just like the prizefighter Mike Tyson. I dismounted from the vehicle and as I approached I at first think he was shot or at the very least stabbed. I interviewed him and he said he was all right. He said some dude just cut him with a box cutter in the mall. I called for an ambulance and another Trooper. Soon two troopers arrived and by this time I knew this kid was all right, he just needs some medical help. I take one of the troopers with me and we go into the mall to look for the subject who did the stabbing.

We located him on the other side of the mall sitting in an ambulance. The medics were all out of the vehicle. The Trooper with me said to the guy, "You, come over here!" The guy looks around, points at himself and says, "You mean me?", (he was the only one in the vehicle) I searched him and found no blade, however the other Trooper located the box cutter in a potted plant in the area where the defendant was located. During a search of the subject, I notice he had a cap on his front teeth made of gold and it was removable. We arrested him for the assault and transported him to station for processing.

While we were at the station, one of our dispatchers picked up what was going on and called the New York City Police Department concerning the subject we had in custody. He was from the city. The N.Y.C. detectives sent back an inquiry as to whether the subject had gold teeth. I contacted them by phone and they explained that a subject that fits the description of our guy is wanted for armed robbery. The one they are looking for has gold teeth. The detective called back and said that our guy with the gold teeth was very possibly the robber they were looking for. Later when we returned to the mall to interview witnesses we found that the two injured subjects had gone in and out of stores while they were chasing each other. One of the clerks told me some of the customers were on their knees praying they were so scared. In one of the stores, they had pulled shelves off the wall to use as weapons during the fight. Our final stop that night was at the emergency room of a local hospital to see how badly our complainant was injured. The doctor was still sewing him back together. He needed over one hundred stitches to close the wounds.

* * *

Another case that Trooper Schultz and I worked on in the mall occurred when I stopped in to talk to the loss prevention officer about a pending case and Schultz was there off duty talking to the security officer. She was telling him about a subject that was ripping off the store at that moment. As she was talking, I looked over her shoulder at the TV screen on the wall and I saw a thief filling a large shopping bag with clothing. I yell, "Look!" She spotted the guy and said, "That's him!" Then she ran out through the store. Schultz and I went to the parking lot entered my vehicle and started after him. All of his chases previously were on foot, but we introduced a vehicle to it. When we spotted the subject, he was sitting on the guide rail with a bag of stolen property on the ground in front of him. We came up on him and he could not see us because it was pitch black out. When he sees that it is a troop car, he stands up and I yell, "If you move I'm going to shoot you in the head!" He stood still and put his hands up. We got him to the road and then handcuffed him and processed him at the station. We recovered all the property and found that he was a professional thief with a very long arrest record all along the east coast.

* * *

On another occasion, while I was sitting in my perch using the binoculars at the mall, I spotted two males in a car enter the far end of the lot. One of them got out of the car a long way from the mall building and the car kept going through the parking lot. I watched the man on foot and noticed he kept stopping and looking into the parked vehicles. The subject in the car continued around the building and drove out of sight. Now I feel I have enough reason to detain the subject on foot but I need help to locate the one in the vehicle. I get on the air trying to locate another troop car close to me and the only one I can get is my Zone Sergeant Mike O'Brien. When he answered, I explain what I have and he is very good about joining me in the case. I gave him the last location of the bad guy in the vehicle and within a few minutes he located him.

I get to his location and file check the vehicle for wants and come up with an active File 1 stolen vehicle out of Schenectady, NY. Both of the occupants are members of the five percenters, a radical black group that believes the names they were born with are slave names and their real name is the one they chose to use now. You can bet the name chosen will have a couple of x's in it. I thanked my former partner, the zone sergeant for his help and took my catch in to be processed at the Guilderland Station.

* * *

Another Crossgate's Mall case I was involved with was a counterfeiting case I received from the Guilderland Police Department. They requested assistance for a man in the shopping center who was passing one hundred dollar bills. The officer gave me a good description of the guy. It was summertime and the temperature was about eighty-five degrees. The subject was reportedly wearing a large dark brown heavy sweater. I pulled up to one of the entrances and spotted the man. I got out and started to approach the man when he turned to run. As I caught up to him he started to fight with me to get away. I got him in just the right position for a hip toss. I tossed him and he must have gone about ten feet before he landed, but when he landed, all the fight was gone out of him. His pockets were full of counterfeit money. Investigator Dennis Moesner arrived soon after to assist in the case.

* * *

On another shoplifting case in the mall I was given

a description of a woman shoplifter who had fled the scene wearing pink slacks. I started looking for the woman in the parking lot and did not spot her. Then I noticed a small woman in a blue dress as I got close to her I could see she had something stuffed under her skirt. What she had done was roll up her pants leg to hide her Identity. I arrested her and put her in the car and she told me she had TB. I did not believe her but I still had to make all the notifications and contact the county jail and advise them of what I had while in route to that location. I also had to tell the Albany County Health Officer who directed me to go for TB tests. All because that little witch wanted to steal clothing.

* * *

Some of the people we had to deal with were very dumb. One time I had a bad check case in Albany. When I interviewed the person whose name was on the checks, she told me they were stolen from her house. I told her the person who cashed the checks used your driver's license to cash the checks. She told me that her license was also stolen. I pointed out to her that she just used her Driver's license to identify herself to me. Then she admitted writing the checks.

Keough and The New Trooper

Around this time, I started riding the post in Guilderland with a new trooper. He is still on the job so I will not name him here. When he first started on the job he went to the "Guns 'R Us Store" and bought a few extra guns and one night with me he felt he had to use some of them.

We get a call from the dispatcher about a lady who sighted an injured fox on Foundry Road in the Town of Guilderland. We checked the area and could not find it. The dispatcher then contacted us and told us the woman wanted to meet us at the Guilderland station. She was waiting for us upon our arrival. She said she just did not want to go home without doing something for the fox. I advised her that we did not have any fox parts and there was no place to get it fixed if we found it. I told her the only thing we are equipped to do is to kill it if it is suffering.

I put her in our car because it was quicker than following her around. We got to the area and she sees it. I stop the troop car and start to exit, but the new trooper is already out of the car and has his gun in his hand. We were carrying the "hand cannon"; a .357 Magnum revolver. He fired his first right off the bat and we got the full effect of the round discharging including a three-foot flame and a deafening noise. The fox also got the full effect and decided this is not a good place to rest and he started to run, but both of its back legs were broken and all he could do were circles. Realizing he missed, the new trooper started to fire more rounds quickly. Maybe he thought I was going to blow his target away. Before you can blink twice all remaining five rounds were in the air and hunks of blacktop are flying up. But the fox is still going in circles. New trooper is going backwards trying to load his revolver with a new load of six using a speed loader. I draw my revolver lower the muzzle and fire one round. It strikes the fox in the chest and blows him off the road all in one motion.

The best thing that happened was when the woman said, "Boy, you shoot a lot better than him!" We take her back to her car and continue our patrol. New guy says, "Jim, I hope you can keep this to yourself!" I did until we stopped for coffee and I was just bursting to share it with someone. I told this new trooper that this was too good not to share, so I put out the word about the poor fox. This new trooper and I became very good friends and still are to this day. We do not do much shooting together anymore though.

* * *

We had other cases together. I remember one involved a stolen vehicle from the southern part of the state. We

148

picked it up occupied in the Crossgate's Mall parking lot while on patrol.

Another case is when he and I were riding on I-890 in Schenectady County and we found an intoxicated female in a vehicle all alone. We attempted to remove her from the vehicle to continue with the DWI arrest and when she got out of the car, she wrapped her arms around my partner and fell asleep standing beside the vehicle. She was as pretty as a girl can be and we did our job and got her to safety.

Keough and Schultz

Trooper Schultz did a great job assisting the merchants at Crossgate's Mall, but the Division of State Police did not want him spending a lot of his time there because the bosses felt they could not supply Troopers for all the shopping malls in New York State. While he worked it, he did very well and had many criminal arrests there.

On one of our night patrols Schultz and I had a complaint at the Ramada Inn, a nice motel in our patrol area. Schultz was driving and when we get to it, we find out it is a wedding party and one of the stupid members of the wedding party was mad at his wife, a pretty girl in a gown. He punched her in the face and when she landed on the floor he kicked her twice. Schultz in a very nice way told the man he should get the asshole of the year award and this made me feel very good. This domestic assault occurred before the law was changed and at that time the complainant had to request the arrest of the defendant. She did not want to sign a complaint, so our hands were tied.

* * *

During one of his cases, he was on foot outside the buildings when he spotted a known shoplifter dragging large black plastic bags on the ground behind her as she walked through the parking lot. She was looking at him and was obviously trying to get out of the area. He yelled for her to stop which just encouraged her to go faster. Schultz was very fast (high school track star), but she dropped the bags and Schultz stopped to secure the property and he had to let her go. She got away, but he got the property back.

A few months later I had to transport prisoners from the jail to the court. One of the prisoners was a female arrested for a shoplifting offense. We were in a room waiting for the court to call the names and Schultz stopped in for one of his cases. As soon as he entered the room, she starts watching him like she was a little mouse and he was a hawk. As soon as he left the room she asked me if I knew that Trooper. I answered yes and gave her his name. She replied, "He sure can run!" She had the advantage over Schultz because he was running for his job but she was running to stay out of jail. She had a very large rap sheet.

* * *

When Schultz and I were working the midnight shift, we checked Crossgate's often late at night because the wild animals were out in force. One that I thought was usually hard to find but not so at the mall was the wild

151

coyote. While we were in the mall in the early AM, one of the old timers walking inside started telling me about the sick looking dog he had been seeing. I let him know what it was and he was shocked. Once in a while we would get one in the middle of the parking lot and he was unable to get away because we could just turn the wheel and get in front of him then he would sit and look us up and down. We never hurt any animals while doing this. It was just fun to look at them.

* * *

When Willard Schultz and I ended up in the same car which was quite often, we used to tease each other constantly. He liked to stop and eat at 3AM and I would always try to make believe I was not going to stop. I would drive by the eatery only to u-turn and come back. One night at the Wendy's on Route 20, we were on a break and the town Police Department came in for their break. When we got ready to leave, the town guys found that someone had stolen the radar unit off the side of their car. Schultz wanted me to drop him off at a location close to the college. I did what he wanted and kept looking for the people who committed the larceny. Within a very short time, Schultz called reporting he had the subject and the stolen item. He just turned him over to the Town Police. If a Trooper had lost something like that they would have wanted to skin him without a doubt.

152

* * *

While Schultz and I were on nights, we kept running into a subject from Schenectady, N.Y. He had a crew that he was always with. The subject drove an old Chrysler Imperial and the vehicle was old enough to be a vehicle you would remember. We both reported for work on the afternoon shift and were ordered to report to the Village of Altamont for a homicide that night. There was a command post set up in Altamont. We both checked in at the command post and John Caulfield, a BCI man, was the only one present.

Caulfield advised us of what they had on the murder and it was not much. Schultz and I both realized, it was the crew we had been involved with on the night patrol the previous week The subject that owned the large square car they were looking for was recorded in the station blotter for a DWI arrest. Looking that up would give him the address they needed for the suspect. When we checked in with John he told us we could not leave the Command Post unattended and he was getting ready to go out. We had to watch the Command Post and not report our information. We did not know it at the time but he wanted to run with the info we had given him.

The defendant was arrested and committed to the

Albany County Jail. One of the things that I liked about the case was the crime scene had to be guarded twenty-four hours a day seven days a week. I volunteered for the job and was assigned two nights of overtime. This involved sitting on a couch watching films on the VCR until you were relieved. The night patrol stopped in on occasion and brought me a coffee and the Sheriff's office patrol also stopped at times.

* * *

Then it was back to my post in Guilderland riding the midnight shift with Willard Schultz. One of the nights we are riding he yells "STOP THE CAR!" I slow down and I am trying to see what he wants me to stop for and he yells again, "STOP THE CAR!" I stop and I am still looking around trying to figure why he wants me to stop as there is nothing in the road when he suddenly jumps out of the car and starts to take his clothes off! Now I think he has finally gone nuts and he yells that his pepper gas has gone off in the case and had emptied its contents into Willard's shirt. Now I had to take him to the station to change his clothes, but for a while, I was thinking of shooting him!

* * *

At Christmas each year Willard Schultz and I would

154

get together and dress as Old Saint Nick and visit the families of Troopers who worked in our station. We always had a good time and I think the kids did too. Willard Schultz became very close to me over the years and I did not realize how close until my wife came down with cancer and was dying. Schultz showed up every night at the hospital and helped in any way he could. My wife Blanche passed away at the age of fifty-two. She was diagnosed on November 2, 1993 and passed away December 9, 1993, the day before my youngest son turned 18. My youngest daughter was 16. My oldest daughter was 21 and was married just a month before the diagnoses. My oldest son was 23. I was left with four children, and two of them were still in high school. We survived despite the burnt spaghetti and laundry malfunctions. Now three of them are teachers and one ended up working as a Trooper out of Princetown. I have other friends that are as close as Schultz and I feel blessed for all of them.

Off Duty Arrests

One of the things I did not mention were off duty arrests. I did make them when I believed they were necessary. In one incident, I was out in front of my house playing volleyball with my kids and I saw a vehicle pass the house that was going very slow. I said to myself, "Is that guy all right?" He drove on, so I did not take any action. A short time later, he came back and pulled into the yard. I could see him up close and there is no doubt in my mind that he is intoxicated. I had a Troop car parked on the lawn because as a dog handler, I took the car home each night to respond to night calls. I activated the radio and called for a patrol to come and get the drunk off my lawn and they did.

* * *

On another day I was going to Schenectady on Route 146 just north of Route 20 when the car in front of me ran off the right side of the road, lost both hubcaps and kept going without stopping. The operator just continued to the Tip Toe Inn. I watched the vehicle go through the red light in front of the Inn. It struck a new pickup truck that was going through the green light and continued without stopping. I was trying to get close enough to the car to record its license plate when it stopped for a red light. Another car was now between us, so I got out of my car and started to walk up to the bad guy. Apparently, he saw me and he took off. I went back to my car and turned the corner where the bad guy did and I saw him in a parking lot with his lights off. I pull up close and got out with my gun in my hand. When I got close enough, I realized there were two teenage girls in the car. I showed them my shield and told them they would have to come with me. This occurred in the parking lot behind Mahoney's Hardware on O'Dell Street. One of the girls was holding a large glass bowl full of coins. She said all this money is mine. I replied, "I know it". I ask a local to call the police he replied, "I ain't got no phone".

I put the girls in the back seat of my personal car and started down Albany Street into the City of Schenectady where I ran into a city Police unit. She took the girls off my hands and requested I go to the PD station in the city. When I got there, they advised me the girls had just stolen the car, broke into a residence and stole the money. The theft occurred in the Village of Scotia and the Village PD wanted a statement from me.

* * *

The last off duty arrest that I can think of occurred when I was on a walking kick in Crossgate's Mall. I was walking when I notice a young girl leaning against the wall in front of one of the stores. Inside the store within a few

157

feet of her, another girl was shopping and removing items from the rack to look at. Every time the sales girl inside the store turned slightly, she passed items to the girl outside the store. The girl by the door stuck them under her clothing.

I walked over to one of the stores that had a phone and I called the barracks to start a unit to my location. I then walked across the mall, identified myself to the girl outside and arrested her. As soon as her friends saw me talking to her, they wanted to know what was going on saying this must be some mistake. I told them she only has to go to the station for a few minutes, but she will need a ride. I asked them if they would be able to help her, and they were. Trooper Khachaturian arrived and he took the prisoner off my hands. We went to the station and when the friends arrived outside the station, I asked the operator for his license. He did not have one and the car contained the rest of the property they had stolen before I ran into them. They were soon separated from their ill-gotten gains.

Keough and Foster

On a patrol with Jim Foster in Guilderland, we ended up on the Northway approaching a subject on foot. It was a violation to be a pedestrian on an interstate highway. As we got close to him, I saw he was trying to put something in his mouth. I grabbed him and suddenly I was hit in the face very hard. I was very angry to think that this man would strike me and it was quite a punch. I choked him out and took the drugs he had in his mouth. I then got up and I told Foster that guy could really punch. Jim told me the bad guy did not hit me it was him. I must have walked into it. Foster went on to become a Sergeant in my station. That was the first and last time he ever punched me! Thank God.

Keough and McDonald

On a midnight patrol with Trooper Drew McDonald on I-890 in the City of Schenectady, I was driving and we ran a special file check on the license plate of a vehicle alongside of us in traffic. It came back negative; no wants or warrants and we continued our patrol. About five minutes later, they call and ask us if we still had that car. We replied, "negative" and they advise us that the Troy police department just sent a Teletype message advising that the license plate we just ran has been reported as a stolen car out of Troy, NY. It was just entered into the

159

computer. We exited the interstate and went back to the area we last saw it, but it was gone.

We started to look around the area when the car in front of us stopped in the middle of the road and the operator got out of the vehicle and enters a residence, leaving her car blocking both lanes of the road. We waited for her to return. When she started down the road, we stopped her. I approached her and asked for her license and registration. She gave me a photo license from North Carolina and a New York registration for the vehicle. She told me the car belonged to her mother's cousin's sister Sally. I returned to the Troop car and ran a check on the license and it came back to a wanted person. We went back up to her vehicle and arrested her. She explained that she did not know I wanted "her" license. She said I just asked for any license, so she gave me that one, but that was not her. We arrested her and handcuffed her hands behind her back and placed her in the back seat of the Troop car.

As soon as she was in the car, she started to twist and turn insisting that she must go to the bathroom immediately. We called for a City of Schenectady Police Officer unit with a female to respond and suddenly she no longer has to go to the bathroom. We realize all of that squirming was because she had dumped her drugs in our car. When we got to the Schenectady Police Department, we searched our back seat and found her coke, which we arrested her for. We always searched our vehicle before we went on patrol and anything in the back seat had to have been put there by her. I am sure that this woman had police contact all of her life. She was just the type.

Keough and Coyne

When I first went on the job I rode with a lot of older Troopers and had some good times and learned everything that I knew about working the road from them. One of the best of the old timers was Trooper Robert Coyne. We rode a lot of night patrols together and had some good cases together. In one of those cases, we were going to a personal injury accident in the Town of Knox on State Route 146. When we got to a long straight away, I pulled out to pass a car going about seventy miles per hour. The guy we were passing started to go faster, then slowed down. We went past him and were not able to check him because of the accident we were in route to. When we got to the scene of the accident, we discovered it was very minor and there was no need for a report.

I spotted the car we were having trouble passing pulling up to the accident scene. I stepped out in front of it and signaled for the driver to stop. He takes off and the chase was on! He is now flying. He takes a left turn onto a side road and Coyne is screaming, "TURN! TURN!" I know my car will never make the turn at our speed, so I kept going straight. It is a good thing that I did because the bad guy ran off the road in a field as he made the turn. I turned the troop car around and went back to see that the two bad guys have bailed out. I called for more help and it comes. I ask Bob what the driver looked like and he replied, "He looked like an Italian." That was all he could tell me, but one of the cars we called for assistance was operated by Trooper John Mulligan. He called to tell us he spotted two subjects in the Stewart's store in the Village of Altamont.

We proceeded to the village, entered the store and I could tell by their reaction to us that these are our two guys from the stolen car. While we interviewed them they were making up stories as quick as they could but none of them made sense. Then I found a GM auto key in his pocket. I had Mulligan take it back to the stolen vehicle and he confirmed the key fit, so we had a good capture.

* * *

At one time while I was assigned to the scale wagon with Trooper Bob Coyne we received a radio call to assist the Albany County Airport Security man with an arrest at the airport. When we arrived at the airport we were sent to the main entrance. As we entered we saw an old timer with two young girls who were possibly sixteen, handcuffed together with one set of handcuffs. The security guy is holding onto one girl's hand and they were running in a large circle around him. He was calling them "cow cunt cocksuckers" in a very loud voice. I got a hold of the girl on the end and we drag them over to the side. We had about forty people who had put their bags down and were watching the spectacle.

The security man was introduced to me as a retired member named Mike. He continued to call the girls "cow cunt cocksuckers." He also has a large bite on his hand that was bleeding and he kept showing it to me, insisting that I must have something in my Troop car that we can put on this dangerous bite. Soon a couple of other people appear who were from social services and had been transporting the girls by airplane back to New York City for some criminal case they had pending. Now I take the old man out to the Troop car open the trunk and show him I did not have a kit in it that said Bite Kit on it. I would like to kick the social services people in the ass for not helping the old man with the wild kids, but I can't do that so they all go on and do what they were doing.

* * *

At one time the Zone Commander asked me to show Bob how to run the scales as he had just transferred onto the scale wagon and had never run them. He wanted

163

me to help him out for a while and I agreed he should have some help. The very first time we worked together, he told me to stop a truck. It was a single axle tractor-trailer and I could tell by the springs it was empty but he still insisted we weigh it. I went along because he was at least ten years senior to me so I had no choice. We checked it and it was empty. Bob had a hard head but also a heart of gold and he was a very hard worker.

* * *

Another incident we had was on the Northway in the Town of Colonie. We are heading south bound and we come upon a group of Muslim men on the side of the highway. In full view of the passing motorist they are urinating on the road. Bob got out of the vehicle and started screaming at them saying "What in the hell are you doing? I'm going to lock you all up! Cover yourself you God Damn fools!" They all just continued to piss. I could tell they did not speak English. Bob was as red faced as I have ever seen him, but soon we got everything straight and they went on their way and promised not to piss on the highway anymore.

* * *

We were once riding patrol on the night shift in Guilderland and had a call for a fight at The Side Door

Cafe. When we responded, I noticed that the combatants were all construction workers and not one was under two hundred pounds. As Coyne goes in the door he turns to me and tells me to stay in the doorway. I do as I am told and expect to be using the nightstick I am carrying. Bob grabs one of the parties involved and pulls him over to me and goes back in for another. I have a large man now and he is coming with another one. When I got up to three the first one turns and tells me that Coyne has been hassling him for twenty years and hope he does not arrest him again. Now I know these guys are afraid of my partner because of past contact but in this case he just sent them home.

* * *

I could almost forgive him for stretching out my arms on the ambulance calls we made. Bob was very friendly with one of the ambulance girls and they were always short of people to work the ambulance on the night shift. Bob and I helped out as much as possible and more than I wanted to. One of the calls we went on had a patient who weighed at least three hundred and fifty pounds and he was on the third floor. The stretcher had Bob on one end and me on the other. The ambulance crew that night was all female. As we were going down the hall with the stretcher to the next floor, one of the girls got in a bad spot between me and the wall. I tried to reach around her and get her past the stretcher and when I started to push her thru the opening I realized I had her whole breast in my hand. I just kept pushing and she got clear. That was my only reward for the night and we finally got the man to the area of the ambulance and we could go back on patrol.... Thank God. We were the only patrol in that town but we assisted that ambulance whenever it needed help, (I did not molest any other female attendants). I gave up at one.

Keough and Mitchell

While working out of Guilderland on the afternoon shift I heard a call of a burglary in progress in the Town of Clifton Park. I was aware that they were having quite a few break-ins in that area in the daylight hours. I contact Trooper Bruce Mitchell and he advised me he is in route via the Northway. I told him I was also in route via Rte. 9. Both roads run north/south and it was believed one of those roads would be the burglar's escape route. We had a slight description of the car to go on. We were in the area only a short time and Bruce called me reporting he thought he saw the guy southbound on I 87. I got to his location about ten minutes later and he had the guy stopped.

On the dashboard of the defendant's car was a radar detector. Bruce's troop car had a radar unit in it and it was turned on. The burglar used the radar detector to avoid the police so he was slowing down and driving carefully. It was a good thing we had slight description of the car or we might have lost a good arrest because of the radar detector. When Bruce spotted the guy, he was trying to hide in the mall with his car because the radar detector had let him know there was a police car ahead. As luck would have it, he was arrested and many cases were closed.

Keough and Ennis

I worked with another old timer who was always good to the job. He always put in a good day's work. His name was William Ennis. When he joined the Troopers, they were still wearing spurs. Everyone referred to him as Willie. The Zone Commander used to let Willie pick his partners when he was on the truck scales. He picked me and we worked together for a solid year. I enjoyed working with him very much. He was a good man. When I was picked by Trooper Willie Ennis to assist him with the scales detail for trucks I learned quite a bit about trucking and laws pertaining to the big rigs.

* * *

Once the Zone Commander pulled up alongside of us to talk to Willie. He asked if we both had our seat belts on. It was a strict regulation that all members should wear seat belts when in a division vehicle. The vehicles only had two belts in the front seat. Willie replied, "Yes sir we always wear our belts!" The Lieutenant smiled and said, "Pull the extra belt back in the car; it's hanging out the door." He then drove off with a big smile. After Willie put on thirty years as a uniform trooper, he went into the BCI for a few years before he retired.

* * *

At one time, Albany PD had a captain named Herb Devlin. He was a terror at times. My first encounter with him on duty was when I was riding with Willie Ennis and the Albany Police Department was investigating a triple homicide that occurred on the state campus at building twelve. That is the building closest to the State Police Academy. As Willie and I pull up to the Captain, Willie says, "How you doing Captain?" His reply was, "Willie I paid three dollars for these chickens I am an Inspector now". Willie replied, "I'm sorry, I didn't know Inspector" and they both laughed.

The captain filled us in on the case in building twelve. A man who was employed in that building had wrapped a rifle in wrapping paper and brought it to work with him and once he was ready, he unwrapped the gun and started shooting. He killed three people and then entered the stairwell. Two officers from the Capitol Police were in the stairwell with him when he committed suicide. They were on different floors but he could hear them coming on the stairs. At the post, the deceased was found to be wearing ear plugs. Willie had been sent to see if the captain needed any help, but the captain said he was OK and he already had some State Police ID men from Troop Headquarters, so we left to resume patrol.

*　*　*

At one time when I was assigned to the truck scales Willey Ennis and I were watching traffic on Central Avenue. A sedan with a few young men in it stopped in the same lot on the other end, got out and opened the trunk. They were looking at something in the trunk. Just then, another vehicle enters the lot and stops. Two young men get out and start looking into the trunk of the first car. I tell Willey I am going to take a look at what they have in the trunk. We pulled right up on the open trunk and I saw cassette players from the dash of an automobile in the trunk. Now one of the people realize it is a police car and slams the trunk, but I already saw them.

I get my crowbar from the trunk and advise them I can open the trunk if they cannot. I take all four of the units out of their vehicle and examine them. We ended up finding one owner and arrested all the people in the car for possession of stolen property. We returned the unit to the man it was stolen from. It was an unusual case for a scale wagon to be involved in but it worked out all right.

* * *

Coyne and Ennis were the two Senior Troopers out of Loudonville and one time I noticed a couple of dents in the heel of Ennis's shoes and I asked him what they were from. He told me that is what spurs did to the leather of the shoe when you wore them. He went on to tell me that when he first came on the job everyone wore spurs. They were hard to walk down stairs while you were wearing them as they stuck out behind each foot and hooked on the stairs, but he learned how after a few falls. The equipment of the old time troopers was a lot different from what they have now.

Hash Arrest

I was working in Loudonville at Troop Headquarters and driving thru the Guilderland patrol area on my way to work in a marked State Police car. I spotted a vehicle going in the opposite direction with an expired inspection sticker. I turned around and stopped the vehicle. When I approached the vehicle, I noticed that both the operator and the female passenger were wearing robes similar to those worn by a Buddhist monk. Both garments were brightly colored. As I was checking the operator's license, I observed a narcotics implement on the front seat; a Hash Pipe. I obtained the item from the operator and for safety's sake had the operator pull into the parking lot of the State Police station which was about fifty feet up the road.

The operator had admitted to having more drugs in the vehicle. At the station we opened the trunk and found about seven pounds of hash. It was straight from India and looked like a baseball. There were eight of them. Each package had the maker's fingerprints on the outside. I learned talking to the defendant that when the plant is harvested, it is placed in a shed and moved around until the oil starts to come to the surface. Then the worker slides his hand along the plant picking up the oil and forming it into a ball. The man was in custody less than an hour when the drug enforcement people showed up and wanted to adopt the case for themselves. Senior Investigator Martin was the trooper involved with me on this case.

The Northway

One of the fastest and most dangerous chases, I was ever involved with occurred with the Town of Colonie Police Department on Interstate-87. I was advised that the Menands Police Department with assistance from Colonie Police Department were in pursuit of a vehicle on Route 9 in the Town of Colonie and had requested State Police assistance. They were located on Route 9 in the Town of Colonie. I was located on Route 155 in the Town of Colonie and as I started toward Route 9, the dispatcher advised us the vehicle had turned onto Route 155 and was coming my way.

Within a minute, I saw the pursued vehicle in front of me coming my way. On my left there was a large parking lot and I thought I had plenty of room between the pursued vehicle and the first chase car. After the first car went by, I stepped on it, spun the wheel to the left and tried to enter a parking lot on the other side of the road. Unfortunately, at this point, the car engine decided to hesitate, but I just made it to join the chase.

As we approached the Northway, the bad guy

172

entered the interstate going south in the northbound lane. The two local police cars also entered the northbound lanes heading south. I continued on to enter the southbound lanes in the southbound direction and ended up on the opposite side of the center mall as the pursuit continued. I saw sparks flying from the PD unit and the dispatcher advised to watch out because there was some shooting going on. We continued south on Interstate 87 with the bad guy in the northbound lane until we entered the Town of Guilderland. The interstate highway ends at a traffic light at the intersection with Route 20. When I got to the light I turned left and then another left and there I saw the chase terminated where the bad guy had hit another car head on.

I went to attend to the poor woman the bad guy had run into and the first thing she said was, "I'm sorry, I was going the wrong way, I didn't mean to do it." I told her she was all right and she was not going the wrong way, but everyone else was. Then I ended up policing the accident while they took the bad guy to their station to finish the paperwork and to make sure the guy got all the tickets he earned on the chase.

* * *

When the Northway first opened there were a lot of wrong way drivers on the road and many accidents occurred involving them. On a night shift in the Town of Colonie I was policing with another Trooper I believe was Dick Pauley. An accident involving a DWI northbound on Interstate-87 occurred on the bridge over the Mohawk River. We received another call for a possible DWI southbound on Interstate-87 right in the area we were in. We could not use our vehicle to stop the new drunk for two reasons. One, it was shielding the last accident and two, the operator of the first car was handcuffed in the back of the police car. So I exited and went to the southbound side with my large flashlight to flag the drunk over. He kept changing lanes but soon stopped. I opened the door, shoved him over, slid in and drove his car off to the shoulder of the road. I gave him a very quick roadside exam and arrested him for DWI and placed him in the back of the police car with the first drunk. When they were seated, the first drunk chastised the second drunk saying, "You were going the wrong way man."

20 Mall

One of the other malls in the Guilderland area was the Twenty Mall. I happened to have a very good case in that mall. It started when a woman reported her purse missing from a store office while she was working in the front of the store. I checked out with the station on the radio and walked into the mall to interview her. As I was passing a jewelry store, I noticed the counter had two people at it along with the salesperson. They were the only two people in the mall that did not pay any attention to me. I continued into the mall to interview the girl who had lost her wallet. I briefly talked to her and went back to check the store with the two suspicious people in it.

I told the sales girl to check her inventory as quickly as she could. She stated nothing was missing I told her to do it again slowly when she checked it and the second time she found she was missing wristwatches from the counter. The two subjects were at that counter when I came in. I put out a message to the Guilderland Police Department and any other State Police patrols that were in the area. As soon as we started looking around, we located a vehicle in the rear of the mall that had all kinds of stolen property hidden under it. There was property on the top of the tires and next to the car was a full rack of clothing from one of the stores still hanging in place.

We then found the two subjects, advised them of their rights and chained them up. When I got back to the station and ran the plate, it came back to a retired Schenectady policeman. When I contacted him, he reported the car stolen at the Guilderland station to Investigator Craig Masterson, AKA "Bat". He was already familiar with some of the defendants in this case. We went to county court and won a conviction in the case after trial.

Elderly Woman Beaten

When I was working patrol in Guilderland one day, I received a call from the local Guilderland Police Department because they were swamped on this particular day. They gave me a call of an injured person in a residence. I patrolled to the location and at the residence I found an elderly woman who had been assaulted. She was beaten in the face with a hammer and she was suffering from a broken eye socket and fractured skull. After securing medical attention for the victim, one of my concerns at the scene was to preserve evidence. We located a single fingerprint in blood on the refrigerator and it was in good shape.

The victim's home health aide came into the house while I was still there and remarked that she had just gone to the store for a few minutes and was returning. Investigator Dennis Moesner arrived and took charge of the scene. He soon detected blood splatter on the aide's clothing that indicated she was present when the assault took place. After a brief interview, she confessed. Unfortunately, the injuries from the assault left the old lady partially blind.

Motel Parking Lots

When the radio calmed down and things got quiet, I would check the parking lots of the local motels and other areas that might produce a wanted person or vehicle. On one of these trips, I located a vehicle from Massachusetts that had a stolen license plate attached to it. I quickly moved the marked troop car out of the area and returned on foot to record the VIN number from the vehicle. When I got back to the troop car and checked the VIN number, I found it to be stolen from another city other than the one the plate was stolen from. This convinced me that I had a good caper going in the early stage.

I called Trooper Frank Connolly an old and good friend of mine. He agreed with me about the caper looking good and he brought an Ithaca twelve-gauge shotgun to the party. At this time, we had to advise zone supervision of what we had and the Sergeant advised us that the car was most likely dumped in the lot. He suggested we tow it in and follow up on our next shift. He said he would not pay us overtime. We wanted to find the operator of the car, so we asked him to reconsider. He relented after a while and agreed and he would pay overtime only if we came up with an arrest. Little did he know Frank and I would probably have done it for free.

We set up surveillance in an unoccupied room right

in front of where the car was parked. After a couple of hours, a man came out of the bar at the motel with a female and started to get into the stolen car. We got right on him and it turned out not only was he driving a stolen car with stolen plates but he was wanted in three states for various crimes. We got our overtime pay and a couple of good arrests.

* * *

Another case I had in a motel parking lot came after a hit on a parked vehicle with a southern state license plate. I called for a second car and Dave Foster showed up. It was late at night and the hit was for a stolen car. The people in possession of the car were in the motel. We had a passkey and entered the room very carefully. Dave carried a shotgun. As I approached the bed, I saw two people in the bed. A very young girl wearing nothing but a pair of panties and a young boy wearing only underpants. I got a hold on the young girl and she woke up but did not say a word. I put her in the bathroom. Dave woke up the boy. I think he will remember that for the rest of his life. Picture Dave Foster all six foot three of him holding a shotgun waking up a kid in a dark motel room. If my memory serves me correctly, the interview at the scene revealed the two kids had pulled an armed robbery in another state using a pellet pistol. The girl was a juvenile and the boy was her boyfriend from home.

178

Raid on Green Street

When I was fairly young on the job I used to go on a lot of raids and other BCI jobs. One I remember well was in the city of Albany on Green Street. I was assigned to a Senior Investigator named Beckwith from Troop "G", Zone Three, State Police Fonda. Our assigned target location was a storefront on Green Street. We arrived at our location and approached the building. I had my nightstick and I saw the Senior Investigator had a very large sledgehammer. The paperwork we had permitted us to enter without knocking, so the Senior Investigator swings the sledgehammer and hits the doorframe and I see the large plate glass window (four feet wide and eight feet high) start to shake. I notice the molding that holds the glass in place is mostly missing and if it falls out its going to crash right on top of me. From the rear of the store, I see the merchant approaching us and he is yelling the door is open. I reach out and try it and the door opens. We went in then and everything else was good.

Strange People I Met

When working the intersection of I-87 and I-90, you see many strange people passing through. I had a place near the toll barrier where I would let the dog out of the car so he could take care of his business. One time while

179

I was headed to that location I stopped to talk to two subjects walking alongside the road and asked for identification. They produced release forms from a prison down south. I ran them in the computer for wants and warrants. Both were negative. After I was done with them I continued to the spot where I walk the dog.

The first trailer the dog goes near in the tractor-trailer tandem lot has the seal on the rear door broken and boxes close to the door have been opened. I can see the boxes contained sleeping bags. The two guys I just checked were wearing sleeping bags as coats. I went right back to them and recovered the sleeping bags and transported them to the station for interfering with interstate commerce seal.

* * *

Later on in the evening hours I had a small pickup come through the toll barrier. It was from Colorado and there were three subjects in the truck. After I talked to one of the occupants, he admitted to having a pistol in the truck. With a little conversation and searching around, I came up with three unlicensed handguns in the vehicle. I arrested three subjects and confiscated three handguns that night.

* * *

Another time on I-87, I got involved with a pedestrian on the road looking for a ride. As I started to look him over, I saw a large knife in his belt. I took charge of the knife and then I located a small amount of drugs on his person and arrested, cuffed and placed him in the troop car. As I was transporting him for arraignment, the guy says, "You should have checked the other guy on the Northway he had a gun on his belt!" I get right on the radio and called Jim Foster. He was on my post and he answered right away. I sent him after the guy who reportedly had a gun. Within a few minutes, Jim reports he has the guy, but all he had was a holster on his belt with no gun.

* * *

I was once assigned the front desk at Loudonville Headquarters after a leg injury. It was an easy job but in no way was it a good one. While I was on that assignment, I handled people walking in off the street and believe me, some of the desk customers were weird. One of the people I remember was a man who entered the building wearing a suit and tie with a folder under his arm. When I asked if I could help him he said, "I hope so." I said, "What's the problem?" He told me that microwaves were eating his brain. I thought to myself, I have to get rid of this guy, I have other things to do. I try to think of a solution to the man's problem and the only thing I could

181

come up with quickly was to have him contact the Federal Communications Commission (FCC). I told him they were in charge of all Microwave signals. He holds one finger in the air signaling me to wait a minute, opens his folder and produces a letter from the FCC saying they cannot help him with the problem he has and he should try the police department.

At this time the First Sergeant, who has an office next to mine, waves me in. I asked the gentlemen to wait a minute and entered the sergeant's office. The First Sergeant, with a smile on his face, tells me to advise the man to go home and take the largest bowl he has, wrap it in aluminum foil then to remove the foil and wear it on his head and this will prevent the waves from getting into his head. I walked over to the man and gave him the First Sergeant's idea and he replied, "I've tried that and it does not work." With that he left, I suspect not satisfied with the service he obtained.

* * *

I once had a complaint to assist a person on a side road and when I arrived, there were two men working on a vehicle under the hood. Within ten feet of them, a young girl about seventeen is on the ground having an epileptic seizure. The men ignored her completely and did not lift a finger to help her. We called her an ambulance and

182

stayed with her until she was under the control of the medics.

* * *

A women came into the Loudonville station on the night shift when all the bosses were gone and she brought her German shepherd with her. She lived in an apartment and she wanted to give him to someone. We told her to go to the ASPCA but she insisted she wanted to personally give the dog to someone herself and one of the dispatchers said he would like to have it. He takes the dog leash, all the supplies and walks out of the building and puts him in his car. Everything is going good until he returns to walk the dog an hour later. Now the dog is a growling mass of teeth and is trying to bite him through the door. I guess the dog has decided the car needs to be protected, and he knows how to do that just fine. Someone realizes what is going on and they just open the door and let the dog out and then he is fine and wants to be everyone's friend. I do not remember what happened to the dog but I am sure he ended up with a good home as his owner wanted.

* * *

At the time I was assigned to the Guilderland station there was a Sergeant on the Guilderland Department named Doug Laremore. I was assigned on two occasions to assist him with naked females. The first one was at a motel on Route 20. The girl was about twenty years old, very pretty, blond hair, blue eyes, built just right and totally naked. She was also as drunk as a person can get. We knocked on her door and she invited us into her motel room and made no effort to dress or cover herself up. We tried to discover what was going on and she stands up and enters the bathroom. I follow her in and leave the door open. She sits on the throne and does her business when she is done she tells me to get her some paper. I let Doug know, he brings some in, and she wipes herself and stands up entering the main part of the motel. The main complaint was not very much and I think Doug arranged for her to go home.

The second case involving a naked woman was a domestic disturbance at an apartment. A man and a women were fighting. They were both drunk and the women was totally naked. When we arrived at the apartment, the women answered the door and invited us in. I think I ended up with the case because the women showed us her bite and wanted the man arrested for inflicting it on her. It was a large bite and appeared to be human. We arrested the man and transported him to the station. He had some clothes on and when we got to the station, he started talking about his bites. He moved his clothing to the side so we could see them. It turns out he was covered with human bites that he claimed were inflicted by the female that was at the apartment with him when he was arrested. We advised him to contact the town judge and if he wanted to pursue a case against the female we would help him with it.

* * *

Another Trooper that I worked with was John Mulligan. He went on to become a Sergeant and then a member of the BCI. I can remember using him one night when I ran into a nasty girl on Central Avenue in the town of Colonie. I was on patrol with my dog when I observed a young white female run into the road and flag down a vehicle. She was acting in a reckless manner and I was not sure if the two people were together or not. I stopped the car and asked the driver for his license. Before he gets it out, she jumps out of his car and is trying to flag down another car. I keep the operator's license and tell him to pull off the road and I will be right back.

I go and get a hold of the female and that is when she attempts to kick me in the family jewels. She is rather clumsy and not too coordinated so I sidestep her and sweep her foot out from under her and she goes on her ass. All this time she is yelling, "I'm going to bite your balls off!" and other things like that. I had called for another member to assist and Mulligan arrives on the scene. I am hoping that she will continue to be nasty so he will not think I called him for nothing. Now I have her near my car, I start to put her in it and she starts to fight. I open the door and the dog's big head comes out but he misses her. His job is to keep an eye on me and not to let me get hurt and he was doing it very well but I do not want my dog to be biting young women.

Now John Mulligan gets a hold of her and thank God she starts to yell "I'll bite your balls off!" as she is trying to kick him. Her husband has arrived at the scene but he is taking my advice and staying out of it. John got in my car and we transported her to Loudonville Troop Headquarters to be processed. After she was in the station for a while, she started to calm down. We fingerprinted her, took her picture and got her a ride home.

Mail Order Complaints

At times we became involved with other departments, some of which were interesting. I once had a case with a woman where someone kept ordering items from mail order outlets and used her name and address when doing it. She received all kinds of tools and anything else that could be sent by mail. She even had a railroad car rented in her name to go from Albany, New York to San Francisco, California. She showed me a copy of the

186

letter she got from the railroad. It said they were very sorry she chose not to use their railroad but they expected payment in full because the car remained ready for her use and they expected her to use it.

* * *

Another case I had involving the United States Post office involved two young teenage girls who lived close to each other. One girl, to harass the other, started subscribing to magazines using the other girls address. Most of the magazines were Ebony or other black issues. Very soon, the girls were each sending mail to each other and then they are getting mail requesting payment on their accounts. One of the girls called me and I get involved by notifying the postal inspector who sets up an account and sends one of them a subscription to a nonexistent magazine with a special post office box that is a one of a kind. The girl fills it out in her enemy's name and sends it to the post office box. Now he has her dead to rights. She mailed the only copy of that subscription in existence. No one else could have done it so I ended up arresting her for harassment, as the federal Government did not have a section of this nature in their laws.

The Parking Lot Lady

Around this time, I returned from one of the Indian

details. There was a little old lady who took up residence in the parking lot of the Guilderland State Police Barracks. She had resided in the southern part of the state near an airport and I think she was the last member of her family alive. What I got from her conversations was that the State of New York took her estate and she was almost broke. She was driving a 1947 Buick in original and mint conditions and she would become annoyed if you asked her what she wanted for it. She requested help from the Troopers and we put her in touch with a local church group that supplied her with small sums of cash. She went to the local market and brought food back in her car where she consumed it in the vehicle.

She was also dependent on the station bathroom to relieve herself. At some point, someone chased her away and I did not hear from her for quite a while. Then one day I was looking at a newspaper and I saw an article that had been written about how this woman was helped out by a town further up north. It might have been Whitehall NY. I had always hoped she would run off with Bob Coyne, an older Trooper we called "Pa". Granted she was a little older than he was but they would have made a nice couple. I liked it when she referred to the State Police as the constabulary. That was common in the past when the Troopers rode horses.

Charlie Simmons

We had a Trooper at State Police Loudonville named Charlie Simmons and he had a case with an unlicensed handgun that was amazing. At the Turf Inn on Wolf Road in the Town of Colonie, two ladies in their forties were out having a couple of drinks at the motel bar when a man at the bar buys them a drink. They accepted the drink and then got ready to leave. The man follows them out and when the three of them get into the parking lot, the man pulls an unlicensed revolver and forces them into their own car, which happened to be a station wagon. He then strips them down naked and started to rape both women.

During the encounter, he drops the gun and one of the girls picks it up and tries to shoot him but it does not work. During the struggle, the other girl gets behind the wheel and takes off across the lot but she cannot see because the windows are steamed up and she hits a parked car. The man jumps out of the car and takes off and one of the girls calls the State Police. Charlie Simmons responded, searches the vehicle and ends up with the bad guy's wallet. He located and arrested him at the motel. It was a great case and a good arrest. Charlie was later stationed in South Glens Falls and we met up once again.

189

* * *

One time was when the State Police in South Glens Falls were experiencing a large amount of burglaries. I was assigned to assist the patrols in that area with the burglary investigation. I was placed in a position so that I could respond to the burglary complaints as they came in. During this investigation, I ran into a Trooper I used to work with and had not seen in quite a while. I was very happy to see him. I ran up to the state police vehicle he was in, jumped right into the passenger seat and said, "Charlie Simmons, have you fucked any fat ladies lately?" He smacks me and points at the dash and I see the red light is on indicating the transmitter for the radio is on. I very quickly ran my hands on the seat under me and found that I sat on the mike when I got in the car. I released the button and about three other cars called me by name and car number.

About five minutes later the Zone Sergeant in charge of the detail pulled up and told me the Captain wanted to see me. After the detail was over I said, "Ok Sarge, what does the Captain want; the fat ladies phone number?" Nothing happen about that. After all, it was not intentional.

190

Connelly and Arnold

Frank Connelly, Bruce Arnold and I were all great friends and we all served on the Capitol Police together before joining the State Police. One night I received a phone call at my residence from Edward Dandraw. He told me that both Frank and Bruce were just involved in a shooting and they both suffered gunshot wounds. He said he was going to the Albany Medical Center to check on their condition. I told him that I would meet him at the hospital. When I arrived, the place was mobbed, but I went in and talked to both wives and advised if I could do anything at all let me know.

While I was at the Medical Center, I found out the two investigators (Connelly and Arnold) and the Duty Captain, Dan Kelly had entered a residence in the town of New Scotland in an attempt to interview the resident. The subject in the home shot both Frank and Bruce while they were trying to locate the subject, with a 303 rifle. The Troopers were originally called to the residence for a domestic incident. Frank was struck in the forearm and Bruce was hit in the shoulder. The bullet caused massive wounds to both men. At the time of the shooting, Captain Kelly returned fire, but the Trooper that ended the shooting was actually outside the house shooting in through a window. Reportedly, he had six hits for all six rounds.

191

As you might expect, both wives were very upset. Frank and Bruce both were able to return to work. Bruce attained the rank of Colonel and Frank reached the rank of Senior Investigator. They each had long careers with the State Police. We spent a lot of time together during our younger years on the job. At the hospital that night I told them they should have brought the Trooper in with them that was shooting through the window. He was a great shot! Both Frank and Bruce are now retired.

Shootings on the Thruway

One of the incidents that involved my dog and I was the shooting of Trooper Ernst on the New York State Thruway. We received a call at night relative to the case and started to head there. When we arrived at the scene, a Lieutenant was waiting for us and he had a big smile on his face. He explained what happened. He said the Trooper was on patrol and picked up a pedestrian to remove him from the road (no pedestrians are allowed on an interstate highway) and was taking him off the road. He had walked a half a mile north before Ernst got to him. They were driving in the Troop car and came along another disabled vehicle. The Trooper stopped to assist when the pedestrian got out of the Troop Car to talk to the Trooper.

During the interview, the pedestrian attacked Trooper Ernst and was trying to take his revolver. They start to roll around on the ground fighting for the gun when the gun fired striking Trooper Ernst in the thigh. The fight went on and Trooper Ernst gained control of his .357 magnum revolver and shot the bad guy in the chest. The family that was in the other disabled vehicle in the area ran across the field and away from the roadway (they were from the Middle East and not used to our customs but the shooting of a police officer was a little out of norm even for them). The traffic that was going by the scene reported the people running were involved in the altercation with the Trooper. Soon enough people were at the scene to assist the Trooper and investigate the crime. They ended up charging the shooter as a person in need of mental help plus penal law violations. Although he had a .357 magnum round go clear through his chest, he was released from the hospital long before Trooper Ernst who was injured in the thigh.

* * *

I responded to another shooting on the Thruway on the first of the year when Governor Carey was having a party in Albany. A Thruway assigned State Police Lieutenant shot a young man who was caught operating a stolen Vehicle. When approached, the young man started to fight with the Lieutenant during a traffic stop.

The young man died and I was sent to search the scene with a metal detector. We turned up nothing.

The Crooked Lake Motel

Another case that involved a large detail for a number of days was at the Crooked Lake Motel in Rensselaer County. This involved a large number of BCI men staking out a motel that they suspected was going to be held up by a local group of thieves. The investigators had the case under control (no uniform members involved) or at least they thought they did. The bad guys had the motel on their short list of places to rob and they struck on a night the BCI had staked it out. A gun battle in the motel between the BCI men and the bad guys ended with no hits, no runs, no errors and no one left inside. If a uniform Trooper had been at the scene, they may have captured some of the burglars. Instead, everyone got away and the uniform men had to beat the bushes for a few days to take the bad guys into custody.

I was assigned to the detail and one thing they had me do was secure a mine detector from a National Guard unit in Schenectady and bring it to the scene. The ground at the scene of the caper was covered with snow and we used the mine detector to look for metal (guns or other evidence) in the snow. I used the detector and if I recall correctly, we found some handcuffs, but the bad guy's guns that were located were recovered by a trooper walking the grounds after the snow melted.

When I was finished with the mine detector, the Sergeant advised me to bring it to Division Headquarters and turn it in. I did as ordered and one year later the New York National Guard called me and asked that the mine detector be returned as soon as possible. They were having an inspection and needed it back. I went to Division Headquarters, found it and returned it.

One of the guys that was involved in this caper was a lifelong criminal and I had the pleasure of being involved with him again at a domestic disturbance at a residence in Saratoga County. I received the radio call to go to the residence. The woman at the residence advised me that the man had threatened her with a large knife and ran out the door. I went down the road from her house to a pizza place full of people and entered. The perpetrator stuck out like a sore thumb. He was the only one on his knees begging me not to hit him with my stick. I arrested him without incident and the case went before an Albany County Judge as the subject was banned from Saratoga County because of an order from the County Court Judge. He ended up in prison, and I never had contact with that man again.

Indian Reservation Details

One of the duties that I have not mentioned yet is the Indian Reservation details many Troopers did for a number of years. New York State has a number of Indian Reservations. Troopers from "G" Troop routinely responded to the St. Regis Reservation located along the Canadian border between Malone and Massena. The Royal Canadian Mounted Police (RCMP) had to pass through a part of New York to get to an area off the reservation that they were responsible to patrol in Canada. I was assigned a post in front of the Warrior Headquarters and the Indians were observed digging an L-shaped hole that appeared to be for a Machine gun position.

One day a Mountie with the rank of Sergeant Major on his shoulder stopped to talk to me and at the time the Indians were playing music very loud. He asked me what type of music it was and I told him I thought it might be a fertility dance because every time they played it, I would get a big woodie. He seemed to agree with me and wanted to know if I would like to have dinner with the RCMP. I said certainly and I met him the next night at The RCMP Headquarters.

Their mess halls are run by the military but not like ours. I served four years in the USMC and the mess halls they had were hard to take. Clam chowder consisted of tying a clam to a string and pulling it through the broth. I found the RCMP chowder was much better and I actually found some clams in the soup. They had three different items on the menu. The food was very good and I enjoyed the conversation. The Sergeant Major mentioned that he liked to fish in Lake George, New York, which was a surprise to hear as he had all of Canada to fish in.

* * *

Another Man I met at the Indian detail was a guy who liked to bust my balls. We were assigned to checkpoints where everyone would be required to stop and be checked. The first time I stopped my friend he said, "You've got to do some sit ups!" I said, "Yes I know!" Then he would go on his way. The next day he would come through and say "You didn't do the sit ups!"

* * *

The Indians on the reservation seem to disregard most of the traffic regulations like seat belts and car seats. They seem to have a high D.W.I. arrest number. When we were on details near the reservation some were very easy like being assigned to stay in a firehouse for a long period of time. One of the firehouses had a river behind it and the Troopers started to bring fishing poles with them

197

and they would fish all day. Soon the local people started to complain that the Troopers were catching all the fish and the bosses made us stop fishing.

* * *

We also stayed at the hotel in Massena. It was clean, comfortable and the food was not too bad. Many nights I would go to the diner with my station commander Sergeant Ransen Cayola. We had some good times. Rance was a good Sergeant for the Troopers that worked for him and a lot of men avoided problems by consulting him first when something happened. I put in many hours overtime working at the Reservation and made quite a lot of money but I lost a lot of time with my family.

Car Wrecks and Injuries

With respect to driving the State Police vehicles, nothing upsets the bosses more than you having an accident with their car and I did have a few of them. The worst one I was involved in was on the midnight shift and it involved a brand new State Police vehicle I was assigned to ride in Westmere. My partner was fast Eddy Gifford. I was driving because Ed always had problems staying awake on the midnight shift. After we got to Westmere the car was making a slight growling noise, so I returned to the State Police barracks in Loudonville. My intentions were to exchange the vehicle for another. When we got to Loudonville, I fooled around with the emergency brake release and the noise stopped, so I decided to continue the patrol.

We started north on State Route 9 in the town of Colonie. As we got to the intersection of Route 9 and 155, a troop car had a vehicle stopped on the southbound shoulder of Route 9. I turned on the left signal to pull in behind them when I noticed the trooper that had been standing close to the edge of the road jumped back. I looked in the mirror again and I see a vehicle in my lane going like hell. I could not get out of his way because the southbound traffic is too fast and heavy. We impacted as hard as can be and both front seats broke loose. We are spun around and the window glass rained all over us. Then we were hit a second time by a yellow checker taxi and the car spins some more. It comes to rest and I opened my door. It still worked and as I try to get out of the wrecked car, a large man puts his hand on my chest and pushes me back into the police car. I try again and he pushes me again. The third time I say, "Asshole get out of my way". That worked and I find myself on foot at the accident scene.

The operator of the first car that rear-ended me is across the road getting his rights read to him as he is totally drunk, unregistered and uninsured. The other vehicle that hit us is operated by a cab driver who is transporting three prostitutes back to Albany. The cab was being followed by a Town of Colonie police car with two Albany and one Colonie detective in it. They were working a case involving the girls and were following them back to the city. The one city dick that I knew came over to me and said, "Nice job Keough". I cannot remember his proper name but everyone called him Buffalo Head. My zone commander arrived at the scene and checked the police car to see if the lights worked and interviewed me in regards the accident. Years later Ed, my partner, retired over the accident with a leg injury. Anytime someone would ask me about the accident, I would say we got hit twice and after the second crash, I woke Ed up.

About three years after the accident occurred, the troop clerk at SP Loudonville called me into her office to show me a copy of the letter the bad guy had written and sent in with his last check paying the full value of the damage he caused to the State Police vehicle. It was good to see him get stuck paying for the damage he caused.

* * *

I was involved in a couple of other accidents but the damage was minor in both of them. One on duty injury

200

involved a broken bone in my right leg that occurred after a high-speed chase with a stolen vehicle on a night patrol with John Caulfield in and around the City of Cohoes. John was the operator and we attempted to stop an older Chevy with two young people in it. The operator refused to stop and ran every red light in the city. He then turned around and ran every light again. John was so frustrated he wanted to ram the car, but I told him we cannot do that because our car was brand new and the car we were chasing was a piece of junk.

As they were going through red lights, we could see the girl and boy in the front seat kissing. After they stopped, I ran up to the operator's door, grabbed the operator by the head and started pulling him out of the window. He kept getting stuck in the opening and I suddenly felt a sharp pain in my right knee. The passenger got out of the vehicle and I let go of the operator to grab the passenger. After we processed both subjects at the station and finished our tour I went home and was hurting so bad I went to the hospital. The doctor found I had broken a bone in my right leg at the knee. I was then assigned to light duty for a period of six weeks. This is when I met the microwave man!

* * *

The next injury I received was on a call at a woman's home in the Town of Colonie. She had gotten into her automobile, started her motor and it made an awful noise. She could hear a cat crying. I got down on my knees and looked at the undercarriage, and I see part of a cat hanging out from the bottom of her car. The only way I could see to get the cat out was to kill it. I secured the crowbar from the trunk of the troop car and two neighborhood men came to the vehicle. I explained to them that I was going to kill the cat by hitting it with the crowbar and then I planned to remove it from the motor. I wound up, swung the crowbar and my hand continued and hit a piece of tin, giving me a severe laceration on my right hand. I asked one of the guys to remove the first aid kit from the trunk of my car and bandage my right hand with it. The guy said, "What are you going to do now?" I replied, "I'd like to hit the woman in the head with the crowbar, but I guess I best go to the hospital and get patched up".

I drove myself to the Albany Memorial Hospital and a very nice young nurse attended to the wound. She removed the dressing the guy put on and replaced it with a damp one. Soon a doctor came in and was going to close the wound when the nurse came back and told him I had damaged my tendons. The doctor said I would have to wait for a plastic surgeon to close the wound. I think if the nurse had not been there I may have lost the use of my fingers.

I was treated by a plastic surgeon and my hand was not permanently damaged. I only missed about two to three days of work for this injury and I went back to light duty on the front desk at Troop Headquarters. The worst pain in the ass of that job was making all the required log entries by hand. I was right handed and that was my injured hand. While I was assigned to the desk, my co-workers used to catcall at me as they went through the office. After all, I was famous! Every time I was assigned the front desk, the First Sergeant wanted me to stay on as permanent desk personnel, but my job was the road and I loved it.

* * *

I worked almost all afternoon shifts. That was where the activity and action were. The last injury I remember I had was in Saratoga County. Moose Morrissey and I were on the explosive detail. We were getting rid of some blasting caps in a dump and I asked to borrow his knife. He handed it to me, and in an attempt to remove some insulation from a blasting cap, I cut my finger. I should have known the knife was sharp as a razor. What else would an ex-Marine carry? He was a good man and I was sorry to hear he has passed on.

* * *

Another injury I had on duty was a broken right arm. This occurred one night as I stopped the troop car in front of the Guilderland station. I got out of the vehicle, dropped the keys into my right trouser pocket, took a couple of steps and fell on my ass breaking my right arm. I got back on my feet but I could not put my hand in the pocket to get the keys for the car or the station.

The lady across the street was very nice and I often spoke to her when I saw her in front of her residence. I went to her door and knocked and she answered I explained that I could not get my keys out and asked her if she could pull them out for me. She backs right up as if I had asked her to hold my penis. Her husband who was also present came over and pulled my keys out. I thanked him and crossed the street to enter the station. I called Zone Headquarters and they sent over Zone Sergeant McGreevy to investigate the injury. We went to the hospital and checked in. A nurse took my blood pressure and pulse. My pulse was around 60 beats per minute. She looked up and asked, "Are you a runner?" She obviously did not look at me closely! At that time, I weighed let us just say a considerable amount! It was a bit of humor at a painful moment. An X-ray was ordered and later on, the doctor came in and said I have a sprain. We left and I went home thinking this is some sprain because it hurt a ton.

I waited two days over the weekend and then I went to a bone doctor who said, "No wonder you're uncomfortable; your arm is broken!" He placed a cast on it and I had instant relief. I think the job at this point stopped letting employees stay working on light duty because they did not want to let the females work on light duty while pregnant, so I had to take a full six weeks off.

Stolen State Police Motorcycle

Another detail I had in Glens Falls involved transporting property from Glens Falls to the Altamont Fairgrounds. At times it seemed like the First Sergeant thought I was a Teamster and had me drive the division trucks to move items from one area to another. Everything on this trip was for the display at the Altamont Fairgrounds. Trooper John Couch was assigned to go with me and to help with the loading and unloading of items.

When we got to the Glens Falls station, John went nuts because one of the items we saw was a State Police motorcycle and John wanted to bring that to Altamont. I advised him he had to check with the duty Captain (Capt. Lovelock had the duty). John called the Captain and he gave us permission to bring the motorcycle down. We strapped it down in the back of the truck and transported it with the Captain's authority.

Shortly after we got to Altamont, I started to get phone calls concerning the motorcycle. The first call was to my zone reporting I had stolen the motorcycle. One Sergeant from Glens Falls told me I was going to have to drive it back up north on my own time. Shortly thereafter, everything turned out OK, but what a ruckus over that motorcycle. John Couch went into the BCI and worked undercover with narcotics units. When I would see him in public, I would avoid him, as he looked so bad.

Hindquarters/Headquarters

When we worked the night patrol out of Guilderland or Loudonville, we had to make a number of relays from the outlying stations in Zone Three, Fonda to Troop Headquarters and Division Headquarters (aka the Puzzle Palace, Hindquarters or the Ivory Tower) in Albany. The relays consisted of mail and reports. I think I might be one of the few people that arrested someone on Headquarters grounds.

It happened while I was doing the relays with another Trooper and I was alone in the car waiting for him to return with the relays. I saw another vehicle enter the lot circle the building and park in the rear. I approached

206

the vehicle on foot and when I got close to it, I observed a male in the back seat who was pretending he was sleeping. I could also see a young girl who was crying sitting upright in the front seat.

I first interviewed the male who had a criminal record. I then talked to the female who had no record. She stated that she had been at a party and the male had offered her a ride home and she accepted it. Instead of taking her home, he pulled in behind the Hindquarters building and I appeared soon thereafter. I believe his record was for a minor sex crime. The girl just wanted to go home. We ended up arresting the male for trespass and some vehicle and traffic violations and we transported the girl home.

The Hindquarters Building was where all the new equipment was issued to the tit-less troopers like the new magnum revolver and ballistic vests. I guess they should have the good guns in case they have to shoot someone through the desks. The vests are important in case someone goes to Division and tries to shoot them while they are sitting at their desk.

Unusual Incidents

A Trooper who at one time was assigned to the same station that I was in ended up being transferred to the Thruway. As I was going south on the Northway one day I saw a Troop vehicle from the Thruway parked on the shoulder of the highway with two or three other cars. I pulled up and stopped. The friend is walking out of the bushes on the side of the road and with him is a man who is soaking wet. The Trooper, Ed Dandraw, related to me that a sailor got a woman out of the water and then I realize what he is talking about.

There is a small pond on the side of the road and the woman had lost control of her vehicle and ran off the road into a small pond that was big enough for her car to sink into out of sight. The sailor had been following her in another car, saw her sink, entered the water and pulled her out with one of her dogs saving their lives. Ed had just come upon them as he was returning to the Thruway from town court. I took the accident case from Ed so he could return to his post. The big problem was the sailor missed his airplane and might be in big trouble with the navy. I told him not to worry I would take care of that. After I sent him on his way with my thanks, I notified the Provost Marshal at his assigned station via telephone and I followed it up with a memo to State Police Headquarters requesting they acknowledge his help in saving the woman's life.

A couple of months later, I was walking by a telephone that is not normally manned and it was ringing.

I answered the phone and on the other end was the commanding officer of a Nuclear Submarine at the New London Submarine base. He called to let me know they were giving the sailor the Navy Marine Corp Life Saving Medal. I thanked him for the call and I was impressed that he made the call himself.

* * *

Another unusual accident I ended up with occurred in the Town I lived in, Knox, New York. It involved a small airplane which crashed taking off from a small private airport in the town. I arrived at the scene and every son of gun in the State Police arrived at the scene including at least two Lieutenants, a Major, all kinds of Sergeants and Investigators and of course me who did all of the work involved at the scene. The supervisors walked around the scene and shot the shit with each other.

What happened was the aircraft went down the runway on the fresh cut grass, slowly drifted to the right side off the fresh cut and into grass about eight inches high. The wheels then struck a stone wall that the pilot could not see because of the high grass. The plane left the ground and took to the air for about a hundred feet then dropped down to the ground, but the wheels were bent and the plane crashed. Both occupants were injured. Both men were educated and well to do. The airplane was

209

owned by a group, and it was shared because of the type of aircraft it was. Parachutes were required on the aircraft and the Knox airport also offered the service of re-packing parachutes. They had just picked up their chutes from the Airport and were returning to the Syracuse area. I interviewed both subjects at Ellis hospital in Schenectady while they were being treated for injuries suffered in the plane accident. I was advised the airplane's specialty was aerobatics which was why parachutes were required when the plane was being operated.

* * *

When I first went on the job, the troop cars on controlled access highways were one-man patrols. The Trooper Police Benevolent Association (PBA) kept after the Division until they agreed to put two men in all midnight cars. I hated them for that because I was very happy in my one-man car. Now I suddenly had someone to ride with and they were sometimes hard to get along with. One of the guys I was assigned to work with made no more than five criminal arrests in ten years. He went on the security detail that was assigned to the mansion for the governor and within a few years he was made a Senior Investigator in the BCI. I was happy as long as I did not have to work with him.

* * *

The one-man car on the North Way had been a good job but it changed when they put two men in the night car. When it was a one-man car, I was working one night alone and the Colonie Police Department requested assistance with a high-speed chase on Central Ave involving a stolen car. Sergeant Casey was the officer that started the chase. Casey was the cop that never left Central Ave. He was always involved in some kind of good criminal arrest.

I arrived in the area just after the stolen car crashed and the occupants bailed out on foot and took off running. I was going west of State Route 5 in the Town of Colonie looking for the occupants when suddenly a young man broke from the bushes and ran over to my car pulled open the back door and jumped in the back seat! He had a severe laceration to his ear and was scared to death. Before I could say anything, he said, "Sir, when Policemen shoot do they ever use blanks?" I told him "No." I contacted the police department and advised them I had one of the occupants and would drop him at the town hall. Casey retired, but I understand he had two sons that are now Colonie Police Department Officers.

* * *

211

My next case I do not remember the Trooper who was with me when it happened, but it occurred at the Ramada Inn on State Route 20 on the midnight shift. The complainant was at the front desk and he had been assaulted. The man was covered with welts and he told us he had met a young man in Washington Park in the City of Albany and they were going to get together at the Ramada. The young man he had met was driving a van truck. He goes to the Ramada and spots the van in the rear parking lot, so he pulls up next to it and the rear of the van opens. Three young men come out all armed with pool cues and start beating him. A pool cue is a very dangerous weapon because they sometimes have a large piece of lead in the handle and may cause severe injury. The Paramedics were at the scene to take care of the injured party, so we went to where the assault took place. I got out and we started to look around and we found a valid registration for a van truck, the same color as the one involved in our case.

We patrolled to the address that was on the registration and there sat the van. As I looked in the window of the van, I saw a pool cue. Knocking on the door of the house brought a lady out and she told us her son was out with some friends in the van and the friends are staying over. We ended up transporting them all to the station and processed them for assault.

One other time I was at the gas pump at Loudonville fueling the vehicle after a C-line shift which was three Pm to eleven PM. I received a complaint from Loudonville that the village Police officer is being shot at in a cemetery located in the village of Waterford. I drive to that location as soon as possible and find the officer in the cemetery in his patrol vehicle and he tells me that an unknown subject shot at his vehicle and the projectile entered through the right front passengers window and broke the window passing through the vehicle and exited through the left front window which was open. The village Officer saw nothing and there was no evidence at the scene at all. I turned the case over to the BCI and it remained a 'who done it.'

Many years later the operator of that village police car was arrested for involvement in a homicide that had occurred long before the incident at the cemetery had happened. I do not remember the disposition of the case.

Trains

At another time when I was going into work I was using state highway 146 in the Village of Altamont and the train was stopped at the railroad crossing in the village. After a few minutes, I figured something was wrong because it is illegal to block a railroad crossing with a train for more than five minutes. If that time passes, the conductor may be issued a traffic ticket. Soon a railroad man walked to the crossing and advised the train was derailed. I contacted my dispatcher by radio and was assigned to investigate the train accident. The required information for a report is the conductor's name, serial number of the engines, location, cargo and things like that. In my thirty-three years of road work this was my first train accident where I ended up doing the required report.

* * *

I had been to other train accidents. One of them involved a woman who committed suicide by train which ended in a gory mess. I also had a dog call when a train operator in Rensselaer County had run over a woman and stopped the train, but was unable to find her. I was called to the scene to locate the woman. I harnessed the dog and started to look for her. There was a vacant residence close to where she was last seen and I sent a Trooper into it. He came out with a little old lady in a green jacket. When I looked her over, I saw that her jacket was ripped and covered with grease. When the engineer saw her, I thought he was going to pass out. He identified her as the women he had run over. I believe she laid down as the train approached and it went over her. The only damage she had was to her clothing.

* * *

We used to have a Trooper named Turner and he worked in the area. He was famous because the Sergeant in his station sent him to check out some fields alongside of a rail line. The field belonged to a local farmer and it was a dumping ground for stolen cars. The crossing used was for the farm vehicles and it was a little rough. Trooper Turner approached the crossing and slowly lets the front wheels go over it. He tried to pull the rest of the car over the rails, but it would not go. He then tried to back out and it would not do that either. He then exited and looked it over from the outside. That is when he heard CHOO CHOO.

He knew which way the train was coming from, so he started to run in that direction. The train appeared and went right by him and he soon heard the metals collide. He started to run towards the stopped train. When he got to the engine, the engineer was just climbing down from the cab. He saw Trooper Turner and yells "Thank God you're here. We just hit a car!"

A while after that happened I was standing in line at the State Police Academy and I saw Turner at the other end of the line of about thirty men. I yelled, "CHOO

CHOO, how are you?" He turned around and said, "Fuck you Keough!" Forever after that, he was known as "Choo Choo Turner".

Keough and O'Brien

On a midnight patrol with Mike O'Brien a long time ago we received a report of an airplane accident on Route 7 in the Town of Niskayuna. We had two calls via radio from Troop Headquarters describing it as an airplane accident. We got to it in a hurry and we found a Chevrolet Corvette that had rolled over on the pavement. The only thing I could see of the person was one eye and I heard very strange death moans from inside the vehicle. The vehicle was in a thousand pieces all over the road. It ended up being a double fatal.

When we got to the scene, the town Police Department was already there so they ended up taking the accident report. We assisted with traffic control to get the emergency vehicles to the scene to assist the injured people. A car full of nasty drunks arrived and they all had to get out of their car and get in the way. They were right in the path of the ambulance and would not move out of the way. We had to grab them and push them out of the way. As you might expect, one started to resist and my partner's Irish came right up. We arrested the fool and stuffed him in the back seat of the Troop car. All of his

216

friends started telling him not to worry. They told us we had better not arrest him because they had political connections in Rotterdam and they would get him right out of jail.

When we were free of the scene we transported our catch to the Niskayuna Town Hall to be arraigned before the Honorable Homer Brown, Town Justice, Town of Niskayuna. He was formally Trooper Brown of the New York State Police. He retired because of an on duty Troop car accident that cost him one eye. A fine gentleman if ever there was one. The judge saw fit to commit the violator to jail until his next date on the bench.

* * *

Judge Brown was always able to come out at night and handle any case we had. He was a Trooper when they rode horses and they checked in with the postmaster to have their book stamped showing that they had arrived at the town on the date shown. When he was in the mood, he could tell some stories about the old days and bitch about the Corporal who was driving the car when he lost his eye.

Colonie and Guilderland

At night, the town Police Department used to harass the duty desk Sergeant by driving fast through the rear lot. He could hear the vehicle but he could not see it well enough to tell if it was a department car and that kept him on his toes. At times I would stop at the Police Department and the Sergeant would tell me if I ever see that car speeding through the lot at night find out who it is and let him know. He thought it was a civilian. Some of the Colonie Officers became good friends of mine and one, Joe Olander, who was a Sergeant on the town Department quit, took the test and passed it and joined the State Police as a Trooper.

* * *

Another man I worked with in Guilderland was Ken Cook he went on to retire as a Colonel. One night we had one of our local birds acting up in a bar and Cook and I responded at the bar. Two people told us that this person was very drunk and had pulled out a pistol and stuck it in another man's stomach and threatened to kill him. One witness even told us it was a twenty-two caliber. We left and started looking for the guy with the gun and we located him in another bar sitting on a bar stool drunk as can be.

218

We walked up to him and I don't think he knew I was there because I was right behind him and Cook says we want you to come outside with us and he replied, "Fuck You ". That's when I grabbed him, and the bar stool came with us. I got almost to the door, but halfway there, me, him and the bar stool all went down on the floor. I had never seen anyone that looked so scared in my life. I patted him down and found no gun. When he fell, his head opened up, possibly by hitting my flashlight as I had it in my hand. I went straight to the parking lot and checked his car and under the front seat was a BB gun that did look like a twenty-two.

* * *

The town of Guilderland Police Department had a burglary of the place next door to a local bar. It was an auto place and when they got to the scene they found some of the stolen tools on the ground in the bar parking lot and as they checked the area they found a subject sleeping off a drunken night in a pickup with the rest of the tools. The Guilderland Police arrested him and convicted him in court and he got to go to prison and take a nice little vacation. The same subject had been involved with the Guilderland Police in the same area and we stopped to assist. The bad guy lost some of his front teeth and after the incident. I saw one of the Police Officers looking for the teeth with his flashlight and I asked him if he was going to make a necklace out of them but he was not in the mood for humor.

* * *

I received a radio dispatch from Loudonville to interview some people in Guilderland Center. It was regarding a subject trying to enter their residence. I arrived at the residence and talk to the man and women who lived there. They were very upset and they were both in their seventies. They tell me the doorbell at the residence rang and when they answered it, the man at the door told them he was interested in buying old jewelry. They told the guy that they had some jewelry but before anything else could happen the man pushes past the complainant and runs up the stairs to the second floor. The old man tries to follow, but is very slow on the stairs so by the time he gets to the top the intruder is already coming back down the stairs and tells them he left some money on the bed.

The old man tries to stop him but he just kept going out the door and up the road to his car. The old man describes the car as an older large vehicle shaped square. I get on the radio and put the description on the air as soon as I can. I get a reply from Senior Investigator Tom Martin who happens to be in the area saying that he has a vehicle in sight matching the wanted vehicle and will be stopping it on Route 146 near the village of Altamont. I mounted up and was in route to his location within a few minutes we were interviewing the man alongside of the road. Some of the property stolen from the residence is visible on the seat of the car. The man states that he purchased the items and the more we talked to him the better he looked as a suspect. At the end of the interview, the man started bitching about the state of New York not letting him make a living and we should not be bothering him. He was convicted after trial and sent to prison right where he belonged.

About ten years later I was working the desk at Duanesburg station and I hear a patrol unit from the Fonda area checking a name on the radio and it was this bad guy. I contacted the patrol and he said he just had a misunderstanding with some people at a residence. I let him know the guy was a convicted burglar, but the guy was released. The Trooper advised me he did not have enough for an arrest.

* * *

At one time there was a bar and grill on Route 20 in the town of Guilderland called the Swiss Inn. It had wooden floors for dancing, unlimited supplies of peanuts and draft beer. Every so often, the station at Guilderland would have a little party. Members would bring their wives and everyone would have a good time. Banjo bands would play music and old time movies were shown on the walls. One night the place was a little rowdier than usual and the owners employed a man who was some kind of a part time deputy at the County Sheriff's. He had a uniform and a large handgun and was walking around the tables when one of the customers grabbed his handgun and fired it into the ceiling twice. The entire place started to empty out and many fights broke out among the customers. The man who took the gun brought it outside and fired it in the air a few times. Everyone who had been fighting ran for their vehicles and took off out of the lot including the man with the gun.

Now all the dispatchers at the state police stations are receiving calls about the gun having been fired and the fight that had gone on at the bar. The patrols are being assigned to each hospital to locate the injured and the gun and my assignment is Ellis Hospital Emergency Room. I arrive as soon as I can and the emergency room is full of combatants from the bar I search for the gun and take names and address of people present.

One of the people mentioned that a man being treated may have had the gun. I enter the treatment room and the doctor tells me I cannot come in. I explain the man may have a gun and the Doctor walks past me and says go ahead. I searched the subject with negative

222

results and about this time the dispatcher notifies me they have the man who had the gun in custody but the gun is still missing. I return to Loudonville where the interviews are being conducted, and the BCI is involved. The case ends with the subject who had stolen the handgun being arrested. The gun was located so the case was closed.

Hospital Details

Another unusual case I had involved a guard job at the Albany Medical Center with a subject who was a prisoner under arrest for murder. He had committed a double homicide in New Jersey and fled the scene into New York. Shortly after entering New York he ran into a concrete truck on the highway and was in very poor condition in the intensive care unit at Albany Medical Center. Both of his legs were broken and he had all kinds of other injuries. One of the nurses was kind enough to let me know he also had AIDS.

I spent my shift in the hall sitting on a chair watching the poor nurses working themselves to death. They were running from one patient to the next and you could see they were actually panting they were going so fast. I never realized how hard they worked. I always believed the closest thing on Earth to an angel was a nurse and I still do.

* * *

Another assignment I had was in St Peter's Hospital. I was assigned to guard a small girl under ten who had been in her own house when some drug freaks broke in looking to rob the residence. The girl's house was also a drug den and during the robbery, someone struck the little girl in the skull and fractured it. When I first saw her she was sitting up and her father, who did not live with the girl, was using his own sign language to communicate with her. He would hold up his thumb and if she wanted a chocolate chip cookie, she would hold up her thumb and he would give her another cookie. The injury to her brain prevented her from talking.

I had the job two nights in a row and the second night I showed up with two boxes of chocolate chip cookies for her and the nurse took me aside and showed me she already had six boxes from the nurses. You have to love those nurses! I know the nurses that helped my children and I when my wife was sick were some of the most compassionate and kind people I will ever have the pleasure to meet. I had trouble going back to thank them because it was such a painful time for my family, but I sent my daughter in with a Villa Itallia Cookie Tray for them. I was at her bedside in St. Clare's Hospital and all of the nurses turned out to be the best nurses I ever met.

Altamont Cases

Another case that occurred in Altamont involved me coming home from a night call. I heard a call about a hit and run driver headed to Altamont. As I entered the village, I spotted the vehicle that was wanted in the hit and run. I stopped him and checked him out. The operator was as drunk as he could get and under his front seat is a fully loaded nine-millimeter pistol. I arrested him and took the gun. It was registered to the defendant. I take the gun into custody and enter it in the station evidence locker noting its serial number and the facts of the arrest. I processed the drunk as you would any other, and tried to go home again. A relative picked up the defendant.

* * *

I was involved in an incident with George Pratt when I was returning from a night call going through the village of Altamont. I apprehended a young man breaking into a parked vehicle in an automobile repair shop located on Main Street in the village. I grabbed him and he was totally drunk and yelling he wants to talk to George Pratt, the Police Chief of the village. The owner of the car lot must have called George because he showed up at the scene and I asked him if he wanted the case as I was tired and the village was his domain. He assured me he wanted nothing to do with it. I then turned my vehicle around and returned to my station to complete the paperwork in this case.

* * *

The biggest case that George was involved in was a high-speed chase that will be forever known as "The Great Turkey Chase." This chase originated in the city of Schenectady, involved about five police departments, and went through two counties ending in the Village of Altamont. The truck involved was reported stolen. During the chase there was much shooting as one of the Schenectady police officers in the early part of the chase reported gunshots coming from the large truck that was being chased.

George had the honor of being one of the few officers that was filmed by a local TV news crew actually firing his weapon. George stated after the case was over he was just shooting to steer the bad guy away from the village. No one was shot in this chase and my only involvement was one of my neighbors came to my house to tell me she just saw a news report and the newsperson said Troopers were chasing the truck and a Trooper was injured. My residence is only about a half of a mile from the ending point of "The Great Turkey Chase" and it was time for me to go to work anyway so I headed that way to check it out.

The reason they called it The Great Turkey Chase is the truck that was stolen was carrying donated turkeys for Thanksgiving. The bad guy found it, jumped in it and the chase was on. The department that started the chase was the Schenectady PD. Colonie, Guilderland and Rotterdam Police Departments, Schenectady County Sheriff's Office, Albany County Sheriff's, and the New York State Police all joined in along the way. The last department involved was the village of Altamont and Chief George Pratt was in command.

The chase ended at the La Salette Seminary. The area was like a park with well-maintained walkways and lawns. At one time, the area was used to train Catholic priests. The bad guy drove the truck until it wouldn't go any further and then got out and ran on foot until one of the police officers caught him and arrested him. The vehicle, with all its bullet holes, was towed to the G Troop Headquarters for processing. It is not known how many of the turkeys were shot, but the local people came out and made the losses good.

* * *

I had another contact with George Pratt when I was assigned a post that included the Village of Altamont and the dispatcher contacted me through the radio and advised me that someone was shooting a gun in a house on Maple Avenue in the Village of Altamont. Her voice sounded excited, so I acknowledged the call and started up to the Altamont area. When I got to the scene of the incident, George was already there and I learned that a possum had fallen into a garbage can and was stuck because the can was empty so he could not climb out. When George got there, he placed the muzzle of his pistol inside the can and shot at the possum six times missing him each and every time. One of the neighbors felt sorry for the possum and kicked the can over and the possum ran away. The first thing I did when I got there was to cancel any other cars they had in route and close the case.

* * *

One other time when I was assigned to the Altamont area, I had a call to interview a subject who was having trouble with one of his children. When I arrived, I knocked on the door and a man yelled, "Come in." I stepped into the house and everything in the house was knocked over. Much of the furniture was broken and the man that told me to come in was sitting on a boy in the middle of the floor. The boy was in his late teens he tells me this is his son and George Pratt brought him home because he drank a full quart of whiskey. The old man could not handle him. The father told me as soon as

228

George left, the kid went nuts and started breaking everything he could. I helped the father put handcuffs on his son and called for an ambulance to transport the young man to a local hospital to be treated for alcohol poisoning.

* * *

On one occasion, I happened to be driving through the village of Altamont and I was stopped by a construction worker flagman who was letting the traffic enter from a side road onto the main highway. An old man going in the other direction ignored or did not see the flagman and kept coming. He hit a woman's car who was entering the main road and knocked her car onto its side. The old man's car kept climbing onto her car. His tires were off the ground but the wheels were still turning. I got out of my truck walked over to his car reached in and pulled the key.

The old man got out of the car and then I went to the other side of the accident and looked down into the vehicle that was on its side. The driver was a very pregnant women squatting on the door of the car still inside the car. I asked if she is all right and she said, "Yes, but I am eight months pregnant." I told her I would have her out in a minute. I got a coat from a construction worker and passed it to her through a window that was slightly open. I told her to put the jacket over her because I was going to break her window and I did not want the glass to get all over her. She complied and I smashed the window. I called a construction worker over to help me lift her from the car. He took one arm and I took the other. We pulled her straight up and as soon as her head cleared the window, the perfect picture of a pretty, pregnant women said, "Where is that fucking cocksucker that did this?"

By this time, the old man had walked home. We had no problem finding the guy. He lived right in the village and everyone knew him. He never understood that he did something wrong. I saw him after the accident driving a full size farm tractor to the store in the village. I am sure he had problems with his license. Most old timers get revoked if they are totally in the wrong at an accident scene. The Department of Motor Vehicle will take their license to protect the people on the highway.

* * *

One of my neighbors contacted me on the phone once and wanted to talk about an attempted burglary to their residence. He requested I stop at his house in regards to the incident. When I stopped in, the husband and wife were both home. The front door of the residence was splintered and broken and they told me that they were out together and when they returned they found the door in this condition. The husband had to go to work so after he opened the door and his wife could get in he told her to call the police and left. She called the police but she called George Pratt from the Village of Altamont (the residence was located in the town of Guilderland outside of the village).

Soon after she called him she observed a man walking out of the woods behind her residence. The man came out of the woods and to her front door and told her a story about someone chasing him and he tried to break into her house to get away (a great fairy tale). Shortly after the man came out of the woods George showed up, placed the man in the village police car and drove off. I contacted George and asked him what happened to my burglar and George told me he gave him a ride to Altamont so he could use a phone to call for a ride home. I told George I should include him on my report as an accomplice as he assisted in the getaway.

I knew the man's name when I heard it from prior contacts and when I ran a record check I came up with some prior burglary arrest, which I expected. I turned the case over to Ralph Barbone, a great BCI man that worked in Guilderland and he arrested the subject in this case.

* * *

One of George Pratt's officers in Altamont who did a great job on some burglary investigations with me was Tom Pollard. He had prior service with the Albany County Sheriff's Office. He was working on a burglary of a roofing company that was located in the village. The burglars had entered the building and stolen roofing material consisting of sheets of copper flashing used in special expensive roofing jobs. Pollard had come up with a name as a possible suspect and I knew the person as I had arrested him for burglary in the past. I went to the Junk yards in the city of Albany and at the first one I tried, I located our guy bringing in scrap copper and the junk man told me it was new clean copper. I told him I wanted to check his records for the last month and he went along with me we located a total of four slips in the name of the guy we suspected all for the clean copper burglaries. I let Tom Pollard know and told him we should get the BCI involved and he agreed so we transferred the case to the BCI and they did the interviews and presented the case to the courts.

Domestic Violence Incidents

Midnights were a shift for domestics and we had our share of them. One that stayed with me for a long time was between an older couple and their adult daughter. The older couple were fighting and the daughter who was about forty was trying to calm them down. We finally got the old man to agree to accept a ride from us to his brother's house because he was much too drunk to drive. When we were about to leave and the old man says to the old women "Vera the only thing I am going to regret about losing you is you were the best blow job I ever had." He just kept saying it over and over the daughter's face was beat red. Then we got him out to the car and drove him away. He was a class act.

* * *

We had another guy that was a constant domestic problem. His shoe was a size seventeen and the rest of him was also very large. His father had been a police officer and whenever his women called the police, he knew exactly how to respond to the police answering the complaint. He would greet the patrol at the door and invite them into his house in a calm and normal voice. All this while his girlfriend was screaming and cursing at him and trying to find a weapon or something else that would cause him pain. Because of the domestic laws that the state had at this time she would normally get arrested and he would walk. The laws have since changed.

* * *

233

One other domestic case I was involved in was a man breaking up with his girlfriend. He had a new girlfriend but the old girlfriend was very upset and she was doing everything in her power to retain her boyfriend. The case is getting more and more dangerous as she is chasing him with the car on and off the road into the fields. The boyfriend refuses to have her arrested, and after a while, the two girlfriends meet. A large argument occurs. I get in at the end of the fight and now he has her arrested.

I arrest her and transport her to the Guilderland station to be processed and all the while she is in my custody she is complaining about her boyfriend choosing the new girlfriend because she has such large breast. She tells me the new girl is nothing but a pig and so is her old boyfriend because he likes big hoots. At this time, I am fingerprinting her and I remark maybe a little silicone might get her out of her problem. She declines and that was about it until about a year later. I am walking into a Stewart's store on State route 20 and a woman is coming out of the store. She stopped in her tracks, pulled her coat all the way open and says, "Look no silicone". She startled me because I did not know who she was for a minute but then her big smile gave her away and we both had a good laugh.

* * *

Another domestic disturbance I policed involved a man and a women arguing over the lack of a stove at their residence. I went into the kitchen and noticed she was cooking on a hot plate, but the poor man said he was working on it. I told the wife maybe she could give him a little time and she exploded, yelling at me. She said, "I've been cooking on the Goddamn hot plate for fourteen years!" That was one time I should have kept my mouth shut.

* * *

Another domestic disturbance I worked was one of the few times I had a Female Trooper with me. This case showed how important it was to have one available in this type of situation. We go to the residence and the women tells us she was sleeping and she wakes up with a naked man pushing against her and she can smell that he has been drinking. Her house rules were if you come home drunk, no sex. She tells him that and pushes him away and he keeps coming back. She gets out of bed, grabs her blanket and heads for another room. She was hollering at him for causing the problem and as she is leaving the room, she turns the light on and discovers the man is not her husband but her brother-in-law. She screams at him to get out because she is worried that if her husband finds them he will kill them both. She runs out of the room. The women Trooper was right up on

235

questions to ask and all other parts of this investigation. I would have been stuttering and slow on the uptake.

* * *

One rape case that I remember involved a woman who called in from a phone booth and requested to report having been raped. I arrived on the scene and she advised it happened in an apartment. When she introduced herself to me she said, "I am a paranoid schizophrenic with homicidal tendencies and I am also a lesbian." She then told me the man had told her to give him a blowjob and made her swallow the evidence when she was done. I knew right away this was a case for the BCI and I contacted them. During our conversations, it seemed as if she was trying to annoy her partner by reporting this to the police. I transported her to the station and Investigator Connelly responded. I could tell by his expression he was pleased with his new case

Animal Encounters

On state highway 20 in the town of Guilderland, the area was very populated. One night at about eight thirty I was going west in the area of Crossgate's Mall. This was during the Christmas season and in the dark I saw a large thing go across the road in heavy traffic. I thought it may

236

have been a man riding a horse. When I got to the area, it crossed in, I turned up the driveway I thought it went into. Standing in the middle of the driveway is a full-grown Moose! It was huge! I was used to seeing deer on the road and dealing with them but this big fella weighed well over a thousand pounds and was not the least bit afraid of my car or me. He did not run, he just walked into the woods. I called for other cars because I just wanted someone to confirm what I saw. I also called EnCon and they were aware he was in the area. He walked slowly away and was killed on the thruway a few hours later.

* * *

Another large animal I saw in the town of Guilderland was a beaver that weighed about forty pounds. It was on the road in French's Hollow. I was working with Dave Serafin in the middle of the night. When I saw it I thought it was the largest woodchuck in the world but I soon realized it was a beaver. It walked past us within five feet and went on its way.

* * *

One of my calls to answer a complaint brought me to a residence on a back road. When I knocked on the door, a woman answered and she had a rag tied around her forehead. I could see that there was something inside

237

the rag as it was lumpy and I asked her what was in the rag. She laughed and told me they were raw potatoes because that was the only thing that would cure her headache. As I stood there talking to her I noticed there were large holes chewed in the door casings, large enough for a cat to pass through them without any problem. When I asked her what caused the holes she told me raccoons. She told me they do not bother anyone. The entire time I talked to her, I expected something to come out and scurry across the floor, but nothing did.

* * *

When I was in Duanesburg I went to a residence on a complaint and it was a nice three-bedroom ranch home with carpets on the floor. I am standing in the living room talking to the homeowner and something bumps me in the back of my leg. I turn around and their stands a goat smelling my leg. I tell the women "Lady you have a goat in your house." She says, "He's not supposed to come inside the house but sometimes he does."

* * *

At another residence, I went looking for a wanted subject and a very pretty women invited me in. As soon as I entered the residence, it smelled as if I had walked into a cat's asshole. It smelled awful! I asked her what it was and she said her boyfriend, who was not home had a friendly panther for a pet. The panther and the boyfriend were not home but the home had all kinds of damage. The panther had chewed the walls and door casings.

* * *

One time I entered a gas station on a complaint and a large German Shepard came after me with the intent of biting me. The station attendant grabbed the dog and said "Trooper you're lucky the dog didn't get you!" I said "Yes it would be too bad because these bullets will really bounce on this stone floor!" He held the dog a lot better after that. I could not have shot someone's pet but he did not know that.

* * *

Another pet I had contact with was on a raid at a motor cycle club that had pet dogs. I was assigned to handle the dogs because I was a K-9 guy and the dogs were supposed to be vicious. I entered the room first as the dog will most likely attack the first one in the room. This dog sees me and decided he does not want to be there. He runs to the far end of the room and paces up and down once or twice. For the grand finale, he takes a large shit for himself. At this time, another Trooper enters

239

the room from the other side and the dog runs out the door the Trooper opened.

After that, I was on the evidence collection detail. All the motorcycles involved in this raid were towed to Troop G garage at Loudonville. At first, they tried to call a tow truck but they were afraid to tow them so the First Sergeant hired a U-Haul and we drove them ourselves. I believe they recovered at least one stolen vehicle when the serial numbers were checked.

* * *

I was on patrol about a year later and a trooper called out with about six members of this motorcycle club. I joined him in the traffic stop and it was one club member with about six prospects (Jr members). When they were all off their motorcycles I dismounted the troop car and yelled, "Hey I don't have time to stay today but I'll see you at the next raid." I went back on patrol. There were three other troop cars at the scene.

* * *

One of the funniest desk man calls I had when I was on light duty working the desk at Loudonville involved my good friend Trooper Frank Connelly. He called me and advised me he was going to have to shoot a baboon out of a tree in a trailer park in Saratoga County with his division issue firearm. I wondered why he has to shoot the damn thing and whom it belongs to. He advised me the man that owns the baboon is not home and none of his neighbors know where he is or when he will return. Frank called the zoo in New York City and they advised a baboon might be very dangerous especially to children. Frank suggest we might use a tranquilizer if we had one. I tell him I will try to locate one, and within a few minutes I find one not too far from the caper. Soon I have it in route to Frank's location being transported by Bill Truesdale, a fine Trooper of Irish descent who has a very heavy brogue. Soon the gun arrives and they start to open the box it is in and examine it. They figure out that in order to use this type of a gun you have to know how much the animal weighs in order to determine how much juice to put in the dart.

Now assignments are made and Frank is going to operate the weapon as he is a firearms instructor and knows about such things. Bill is going to be the light man and shine the light on the target. One of the people shouts action and the gun comes up and makes a slight noise but nothing happens to the animal. Bill walks over to Frank and says "Frankie me boy, I'm thinking you missed the monkey." Frank's reply was "I held the sight right on its center mass!" Bill says, "Now Frankie boy don't you think you might have twitched just a little? If the gun shoots straight you should have hit him." At this time the monkey comes falling out of the tree and lands between the two Troopers. After a couple of holy shits, they approach the target and find that they did hit the target right in the center and the reason it fell from the tree is because it was as dead as a doornail! After they got done it was found that the dart in the gun was too long and went through the animal's heart killing it. Frank Connelly always stated that it was his shooting that made the difference, but on the other hand, Bill Truesdale claims to be the best man with a spotlight.

About two weeks after this case Frank called me on the phone and told me he has a complaint with the largest snapping turtle he has ever seen and he thinks he might have to shoot him, but somehow he got rid of the turtle without a gunfight or a spot light man. With men like this we can do, anything required involving any kind of critter we happen to run into.

Restaurant and Bar Cases

There were two big cases I was involved in that occurred on the night patrol. One involved a subject shooting a gun off near the Red Apple Restaurant. We both heard the shot but my partner, a Trooper named Olson saw a subject run into a building that was used as a residence for migrant workers. He drove right to the door of the building and we went inside. Olson got right ahold of the person and turned him over to me so he could look for the gun involved in the shooting. As he was turning him over to me, the guy made a break for it. He got about ten feet and I came down on him like a load of bricks. We both hit the floor with me on top. Olsen came flying out of the room screaming which way did he go and ended up as the third man in the pile.

We went back to the area we had started from and found the gun right away and it stunk of having been fired. We transported him back to the station and I was assigned to take an arrest report from him. The prisoner did not care about anything and was giving me a hard time in regards to the arrest report. A Zone Sergeant named Blake Muthic, (I later learned he was a legend in the State Police), came and talked to him for about two minutes and his whole attitude changed. The gun involved was a nine-millimeter Taurus with a plastic handle and it was loaded, unlicensed and unregistered at the time of his arrest.

* * *

One night while riding nights with Trooper William Ropelewski in the town of Colonie we received a call about a subject in a bar with a holstered pistol on his belt. The call came from an off duty BCI member who was from our zone and he told the dispatcher he had seen the gun himself. He gave a really good description of the gunman. Bill and I entered the front door of the bar with our guns in their holsters. We spotted the guy right off. We approached him together, one of us on each side and brought him to the parking lot. The man is super juiced, and once we are outside he starts to act up a little. We have not searched him yet and he goes to pull away. I tapped him on the head with the muzzle of my pistol. He was complaining that it hurt as we got his jacket off and start searching him. All we could find is a case for eyeglasses fastened to his belt. The BCI man comes over and says it sure looked like a gun in the bar. The subject is not upset and I do not think he even knows I tapped him. We made arrangements to get him a ride home because he is not able to drive and we cannot arrest him for driving while intoxicated because we did not see him drive. Case closed.

* * *

Another place we used to receive calls from was the Village of Waterford in Saratoga County. They had a very small village police department. One of the problems they had was the local politics that interfered with the department. When they changed mayors, the police department would also change. If I was working on a burglary case with a police officer from Waterford the next time I went to the village he might be gone and someone else would be in his position.

One of the cases I remember from that period was a subject in a residence possibly armed and barricaded. Waterford wanted to turn the case over to the State Police as they did not have the manpower to handle it. I arrived at the scene and there was a bar on the first floor of the building that was very busy. I talked to the Village Police Officer and most of the information he has is second hand. I enter the bar and call the manager over. I explained to him that the good times are going to be over. I told him if I located the barricaded subject at the bar, I was going to have to arrest him and handcuff him to the subject for obstructing. I asked if he was in the bar. His reply was "Yes. He's at the last seat on this end of the bar." I thanked him and went and asked the other gentleman to step outside. He does so without a problem so ending the case.

* * *

One other bar case I had with their police department involved a call from an anonymous caller. The caller said at a certain bar in the village an unknown village Police Officer was being assaulted. I go there with two other troopers and at the front door the place is so packed we can hardly move. The night sticks at port arms

245

helped. We form into a wedge at the door and I can see at the other end of the bar a man wearing a Stetson hat as favored by the village police department. We shove our way into the place and up to the man in the hat and he turns out to be just another nut with a funny hat on. We turn the wedge around, shove our way out and contact Loudonville and advise that the complaint is unfounded.

* * *

While Mcgreevy and I were riding one night in the Guilderland area we turned around in the parking lot of The Village Drummer on route 20. We saw a man get on his motorcycle with his back to us and try to start it. As he kicks it, the machine falls over as soon as he starts it. He then crawls out from the bike and starts it again. I dismount out of the car and put my hands on the handlebars of his bike. The guy's eyes are open but I do not think he saw me. I shut the bike off and arrested him for driving while intoxicated and towed his bike. I tested him at the Guilderland station and the test was very high. We most likely saved his life or at least his limbs. On a normal patrol we would not normally bother vehicles in the bar parking lots unless they were acting very stupid.

Keough and Werthmuller

Another man I used to work with until he retired was Jim Werthmuller. We worked together as much as possible and we had many good cases together. One of the funniest was a car with a group of young men in it and some roaches visible in the ashtray. He had the kids get out of the vehicle and I was watching them while he was searching their car. All of a sudden, he made a noise like all the air was knocked out of him and he started screaming, "Who put that dead cat under the seat?" He is so wild yelling about the dead cat and I can see it is laying on the floor of the vehicle. The kid is trying to explain that his mother asked him to bury the cat and he put it under the seat and forgot about it. Werthmuller is still wild and is acting like the kid knew his car was going to be searched and he put the dead cat under the seat so the Trooper would find it. While all this is going on, I am trying to keep a straight face. Soon we give him an appearance ticket. He is on his way with his dead cat and we can get back to work, despite my giggling.

* * *

We had more cases together. One of them involved a subject with a seven-foot-high marijuana plant in the rear seat of a Volkswagen Bug. It was bent over to fit in the tiny car without harming the plant. After we

247

brought the plant to the station, the subject was kissing it goodbye and was very upset about losing it.

* * *

Werthmuller eventually went into undercover work with the BCI and while he was doing that I had a recruit assigned to me for the day. I had a very good day with him. I made three traffic stops for five felony arrests and Werthmuller was assigned to assist us with the cases.

On one of our traffic stops on Interstate 87 Werthmuller and I stopped a Vehicle from New York City with four young males in it. The first subject my partner talks to had four pistol bullets in his pocket. He turned and showed them to me and I draw my issue revolver to keep the subjects covered in case the gun that goes with the bullets shows up. When the one subject saw my gun was out he said "Is that gun a magnum?" I answered yes it is and he put his head back and said "Woo We." We did not find the gun and they were soon on their way.

* * *

Werthmuller and I must have checked a few thousand cars together. On one of our other stops as I approached the vehicle from the right side with Jim on the other side, the man in the right front seat threw a small

248

amount of grass out of the window and it landed on my shoe. He was so involved in watching Jim on the other side of the vehicle that he did not know I was there. When I yelled he almost jumped out of the car! It turned out that was the only grass they had so I issued him a uniform traffic ticket for littering and we let them go on their way.

Demonstrations and "Rations"

On one occasion there was a large demonstration in the city of Albany. The uniform Captain George Abare called me into his office to see if I could drive a large bus to transport a large amount of Troopers to the state capitol to back up the Albany Police Department at the demonstration. I advised him if it had wheels, I could do it. The captain sent me to borrow the bus from one of the local departments. I drove the big sucker to Troop Headquarters but that was as far as it went. The demonstration didn't get bad enough for the bus. At some of the demonstrations, Troopers were put in the state buildings and remained in place until the event was over.

Some of these capers were tough because we had no rations or supply units. Sometimes the supplies we were given were useless. I remember bitching about one radio I was assigned. It weighed about twenty pounds and it did not work at all. A Lieutenant asked me how the radio worked so I told him it did not work at all and I showed him by trying to contact a troop car that was in sight of us with no results. The Lieutenant told me to stand by he would be right back. He left for a while, returned and brought a radio that weighed about ten pounds more than the one I had. It did not work any better. I just kept my mouth shut and humped the extra weight.

Keough and Rope

On another case I had with Bill Ropelewski (known as Rope) on the night shift, we are called to a private delivery service in the town of Colonie. We arrived and speak to the foreman. He tells us this story about one of his drivers who works in the Glens Falls area. She was making her rounds and was flagged down by a man armed with a gun. He got in her van and tied her up using some tape. My first thought was the women got drunk or something of that nature and possibly spent some time with a boyfriend. The foreman vouched for the girl and was positive she wasn't lying.

The boss then took me into another room to talk to the girl and I could see her eyes were bright red. Her wrists and other parts of her body were covered with red areas from being tied, and she smelled of chloroform. After very few words from her, I was sure she was not lying. Rope and I went and inspected the van and the smell of chloroform was very strong. In addition, the rear area of the van had many bits of masking tape scattered around the floor so we knew we had a major crime here. I told Rope to contact South Glens Falls and speak to the BCI there. I continued talking to the girl about the case.

Rope comes back and tells me the BCI wants him to secure the van and get everyone's name and they will come down in the morning. Rope and I get together and decide to contact Troop Headquarters and speak to the duty Captain. I make the call and within a few minutes, the Captain has Troop ID Personal and BCI men enroute to our location. Soon after that, we are back on patrol.

A long time after the incident occurred I talked to one of the BCI men that was involved in this case. He advised me about what happened. The woman was overpowered by art thieves who needed her car to commit a burglary or robbery in the Glens Falls area. They were arrested for another incident in another State and they admitted to this case so it was closed properly.

Legend of a Trooper

There is a legend about a trooper working the day shift out of the East Greenbush station in a snowstorm. When I came on the job, if it snowed you had better put the chains on the wheels of your car. That is why every

251

vehicle had a pair in the trunk. The deskman received a call from a resident to inform him that a State Police vehicle was on its roof on her lawn. The deskman being concerned for the Troopers condition asked the women if the Trooper that was driving the car was all right. Her reply was "I think he's OK because he's on top of the car putting his chains on." I believe that it was true because that is the way things were then.

* * *

Other things that were a little different were the Troop Commander always had a large black vehicle assigned to him and any uniform trooper would spot that car in a minute! At one time the superintendent of the State Police was having a little problem with his assigned vehicle and a Trooper from Post 1 of the Northway patrol was advised to report to division Headquarters.

The trooper was James French and when he got there, they gave him the keys for car 41 and told him to run it up and down the Northway as the engine was running a little rough. They believed that would straighten it out. Frenchy, as he was known, takes control and goes north on the Northway and after about five miles, he spots a troop car parked in the mall. He picks up his mike and calls car 41 to the vehicle near exit seven on the Northway. The car answers with car five one eight is on.

Sir Frenchy's reply is "How are you receiving me." The uniform Trooper replies, "Fine sir." Car 41 is off, and the uniform Trooper can start to breathe again. Frenchy continues his ride enjoying a good belly laugh.

* * *

Another case I had was with the First Sergeant James Furphy. He assigned me to drive a large truck to the Airport at Stewart Air Force base. The military had moved out of it and the State Police were going to operate some of the police helicopters from that area. I had to move parts from Albany to Newburgh by truck. One of the Items I was moving was an old military jeep so I loaded up at Albany and drove the load to Newburgh. The truck had a hydraulic lift and a two-speed axle but I think the first Sergeant thought I was a teamster so I took the truck and backed it into a hill with the tailgate down and then I drove the jeep off the truck and on to the ground.

After everything is secure, I start back to Albany with the truck. It is a large gray vehicle but the license plates are State Police plates. Within a mile or so I get a red light and after I stop for the light I hear people screaming and look out my window and next to me in traffic is a van full of young people and one male is bare ass naked mooning people out the rear of the van. I pull my key, step over to the van and pull their keys. I am in a fatigue uniform and I have a gun belt on with a gun. In about a minute, another troop car pulls up and takes the subjects off my hands. They also found some hash oil in the van. I was on my way back to Albany and I think that was the only arrest anyone ever made with that truck.

Keough and Ebel

My station commander was Sergeant William Ebel. He was an old timer and was a good man to work for. On one occasion, he and I were riding in the same car when we were trying to identify a body found in the town of Halfmoon. It was in the middle of winter. This woman was found dead on the side of the road and she had no Identification on her person. I was assigned to work the area and attempt to ID her and the Sergeant went along with me. The first thing I had to do was go up to the Hospital in Saratoga to attend part of the post mortem exam that was being conducted in order to determine the cause of death. When I entered the room the state police investigator and the doctor were right in the middle of the exam. The investigator stopped what he was doing to give me a photograph that was taken after her death to be used in trying to identifier her. The Sergeant waited in the car, which was something I wish I could have done.

As we returned to the area she was found in the

254

Sergeant directed me to a local bar. I told him "No Sergeant we have to do this investigation. This is no time to be having a drink!" His reply as he glared at me was "Shut up you asshole! Take me to the bar because it's the only place we are going to find anyone to interview."

We arrive at the bar and I go in first with the photo in my hand. Inside the bar are two pool tables and they are both being used by a collection of locals. There were approximately twenty-five to thirty people in the bar at this time and every one of them was looking directly at me thinking this is a raid or something else. I hold up the picture and say, "We are attempting to identify this woman. She has been found dead alongside the road and we are unable to find anyone who knows her or can identify the body." One of the locals comes over to me and asks to look at the photo. He looks at it and grabs his chest and says, "Oh, my God Charlie come over here!" Charlie comes over and he says it looks just like her. I say to him, "Do you know this women?" He says, "She looks just like my mother." I ask him, "Do you think this is your Mother?" He says "No my mother died ten years ago but she looks a lot like her!" I would have liked to have choked him, but I know I can not do that. We show the picture around a little and then we leave. They found out the women died of exposure and alcohol.

* * *

255

A couple of days later I see the Sergeant. He is all worked up and I ask him what is wrong. He tells me he is interviewing a woman over poor service on a personal complaint and she is crazy. I asked him what makes you think she is nuts and his reply was that she puts her lipstick on her teeth not her lips! I had to hand it to him that was a very good indication something was wrong.

* * *

The Sergeant was very punctual and arrived on time and normally left on time. Occasionally, Frank Connelly would reach up and spin the clock ten minutes ahead. The next time the Sergeant looked up, he thought he was late going home and he left. Of course, when he got home he knew he was early so the next day there was hell to pay. He would rant and rave but he never hurt any of us, he was just a good man all around.

Justices of the Peace

Some of the Justices of the Peace that we worked with were very nice people who took their jobs seriously. Due to the nature of the job, we would wake them up in the middle of the night and get them involved in a criminal case when everyone else was snug as a bug in their beds. One name comes to my mind in the town of Clifton

Park was Robert Jerome. We used to get a large amount of Canadian motorist especially on the Queen's birthday (that was a national holiday in Canada). They did a lot of travelling. At one time, we had about ten people from Canada in his office at once and they were all speaking French. When the judge came into the room one of the men stood up and started talking to the other people in French. The judge told him in English to sit down and shut up! The judge's wife was also present and she told the judge in English that the man was only telling the people to show some respect for the court. The judge's wife was a former French Canadian who was fluent in French and often interpreted for the Judge during court. In Judge Jerome's court, things were done his way.

* * *

Another incident I had with Judge Jerome was a case with a Canadian motorist arrested for a very high speed on the Northway. The judge almost always would hike the fine for the higher speeds, and he did so in this case. The defendant pulled a large roll of bills from his pocket and started to throw them on the table in front of the Judge. When he was done, the Judge said, "Can you pull ten days off of that roll?" He added ten days to the defendant's time.

* * *

257

In the adjoining town of Halfmoon, the Justice we used was Vernon Sherer. He was also a very good town Justice who was always ready to work day or night. One night I was riding with Richard Pauley on the Interstate night patrol and we got involved with a drunk driver. The man was so drunk he hardly stood up by himself. For some reason we had to arraign him before a judge and it was Vernon Shear. The time was like 3:00 AM and we brought him into the judge's front room to hear the charge against him. As he is standing in front of the Judge, the man is passing gas and it is very loud, so loud in fact that I think the guy is having a bowel movement. I look down at his feet and there is fecal matter all over the Judges rug. I interrupted the judge and told him the man had shit on his floor and asked him if he wanted me to pull the rug involved onto his porch so he would not have to fool with it at three in the morning. The Judge advised me that it was all right he was going to take care of it. Now I wanted to run out of the residence but I had to drag the drunk with me in his shitty pants. The judge started to call his wife to help him with the mess.

When I got outside I opened the trunk of the police car and dumped a case of flares in the trunk and flattened the box out a little. I put it on the seat in the back so the drunk could have a place to sit. The flare box had a heavy

258

coating of wax to keep moisture from getting to the flares. We put the drunk's ass in the box and drove him to the hospital to get his blood tested for the DWI arrest and he stunk so bad we had the windows open all the way. It was bitter cold. The drunk kept complaining about the cold and why don't we close the windows. That is an example of the bullshit the poor Judge put up with in the middle of the night, but he never said a word about it.

* * *

At a court arraignment in the town of Colonie I was sent to pick up a subject from the Albany County Jail and transport him to a Colonie Court for his arraignment. I was not involved with the arrest of the subject nor was I aware of his case but I was assigned to bring him to court. When I arrived at the court I had the subject handcuffed in the rear of the room and was bringing him to the front of the court. When I got to the front of the court, I heard two people arguing very loud in the rear of the court but I could not see them.

They had town Officers in the area so I tried to ignore it, but now people start pointing it out to me and I have to get involved. I get ahold of my prisoner's handcuffs and start to drag him in the direction of what now sounds like a fight. As we get close, I see there are about four women against the front door and they have

259

another woman by her hair and are banging her head against the window on the door, which is now covered with blood. I grab the one doing the fighting and pull her out of the fight by the hair of her head so she understands what I want her to do. Now the town Police are showing up and I can step back. People do not understand that if I had let my prisoner get away, no matter how it happened, I would have been fined a week's pay and censured. All the people in the court saw was that I was letting the fight go on.

Teamwork on a Hit and Run

One of my best investigations that was conducted with the help of two outstanding Troopers occurred in the town of Knox and it involved my seventeen-year-old daughter, Colleen. My wife and I were going to the hospital with my youngest daughter Erin. She was about twelve years old at the time and that night she complained that her throat hurt and we looked at it and thought it might be strep. Knowing that she has to have medicine to cure this, we took her to the hospital. As we enter my home on our return, it was about midnight and my phone was ringing. I answer it and find its Glen Nissen a Trooper stationed at Loudonville. He tells me that the Albany County Sheriff's office had just run my license plate. They were requesting data information on the license plate that belonged on my oldest daughter Colleen's car, a small

Pontiac Sunbird. The only additional thing he could tell me is he believed the car was in an accident on Warners Lake Road.

I thanked him for the information and told my wife who is almost in tears knowing her seventeen-year-old pretty daughter is in a traffic accident. We leave our youngest daughter in her older brother John's care and go out get in the car to drive to the accident. It was about a ten-minute ride. The deputy handling the accident is Dave Romano, a friend of mine and I ask if he has the occupants of the vehicle. He advises me not yet. The scene is at an intersection in the middle of nowhere. My daughter's car is totaled, and has been pushed into the woods. The entire area is pitch black. There are no lights other than from the vehicles passing by, and my daughter is missing.

Then one of the deputies comes down the road and he has my Colleen in his vehicle. He located her at a farmhouse where her and her girlfriend walked after the accident. I talk to her but she is very shook-up and can supply no description of the other vehicle that left the scene. We go home after driving the other girl home.

The worst thing is I have to go to the State Police Academy for one week following the accident and will be unable to assist in the investigation. I report in as required and I tried to get them to switch my week but they could not do that so I had to sit it out. I was able to contact Trooper Willard Schultz and Trooper William Khachadourian to see if they could come up with some information and they both did very well.

One of the things that helped with the investigation is Colleen gave us a description of a vehicle that passed her car just before the accident. She said it was a small pickup and the driver seemed to be very intoxicated as he was all over the road and passed her on a double solid line. Schultz was able to find out the identification of the operator of the small truck and got information that there was another person drinking with him in a different vehicle. That turned out to be the man we wanted and the one who caused the accident.

Within a few days of my return to the patrol with a little help from a contact of mine, we knew the cars location and where it was repaired. It gave me great pleasure to arrest the operator. When I grabbed him, he wanted to talk to the Drug Enforcement Agency. He was some kind of an informant. That man drove into a car with two seventeen-year-old girls sitting in it at a stop sign, and hit it hard enough to drive it a hundred feet into the woods. He heard the screams of the girls and it made no difference to him. He did not call in their location or assist them in any way and left them in the middle of nowhere in the freezing cold in the dark. I did not care who he wanted to speak to.

We arrested another guy that was with him and was interviewed by me during the investigation. He lied about it the day that I arrested him. I went home and woke up my daughter to let her know. No one was happier than me about the case being closed by an arrest. Maybe she was because she hugged me so tight and said "Dad I knew you would get him!" My old partner Bob Coyne would have been proud of me in this case.

Serious injuries and Accidents

At one time the PBA donated new first aid kits for all the troop cars and they were great. I knew when we got them it would be impossible to restock them and the first time I used it I knew I was right. I came upon a serious personal injury accident on route 155 in the town of Guilderland. Two cars were going in opposite directions, one vehicle swerved to avoid a deer and struck the other car head on. They also killed the deer. The first two cars to stop both had young doctors in them and they were both willing to help. All they needed was my first aid kit. I turned it over and watched my nice new kit get stripped of almost everything but it was all needed and no one died so we won that case.

* * *

I had many serious accidents with very serious injuries. At one time on the Northway I had a pretty young lady roll her car over during a snowstorm. When I arrived, I climbed on top of the vehicle because it was on its side in the mall in very deep but light snow. Now I am inside the overturned vehicle with the injured lady and I say stand up and I will help you out of here. She tells me that she cannot move. I waited for the ambulance people to arrive and they got her out and transported her to the hospital. When I got down to the hospital to see her I found out her spine was severed.

* * *

On that same day I was just getting back to my area and I came on another accident. A motorist struck a flagman directing traffic and both his legs were broken. All the construction workers wanted to lynch the women who hit him but as I looked over the scene, I saw how the accident happened. The flagman was elderly and walked toward the cars waving the flag and when he got a truck in front of him, the next car in line was not able to see him. I talked to the construction workers, they calmed down and we finished the accident report. The women who had hit the flagman was an RN and a very nice lady.

Bodies and People Cooling Off

On duty at SP Guilderland I received a call to interview a subject in an apartment about a bad smell in the hallway. I get to the apartment and the smell is as bad as can be. I get a key from the building super and enter the apartment where the smell is so strong it almost brings me to my knees. In the first room, I located the dead body of an elderly man sitting on a chair. The body is starting to come apart as it seems to have been there for quite a while and the smell is too much. I exit the apartment and call for another Trooper who arrives soon after. I let him know what I have and that this case should be for the detectives. First, I wanted to make sure of what we had. I was ready to call them but I wanted to make sure that I only had one body and there was no foul play. I reentered the apartment and checked each room and all the closets and under the beds to be sure we only had one body. By now, I was choking from the order. I had been present at other deaths but none that smelled this bad.

I tell the young Trooper to remain at the scene and I would go up to the fire department to get some Scott Air Packs. I stop in at the fire department and the firemen go along with me and give me two air packs to take back to the scene. I go and the Trooper is still waiting. I had called the BCI prior to leaving. I unloaded the air packs and soon

265

the BCI man arrives at the scene. I offer him the air pack and he says "I don't need that shit." After I brief him on what I had done, he enters the apartment. He spins right around and says, "Hand me that air pack will you?" Soon the BCI were at the scene in force so I left and went back on patrol.

* * *

I was asked to do another check on the welfare of an elderly man who lived alone and had not been seen for a while. The residence was in the town of Colonie and I located it without any problem and was able to enter the house. I located the old man in his bed covered up and dead as could be. The house was very cluttered and had dirt floors. Not too many houses like that in the town of Colonie.

* * *

Another case I had involved some students locating the body of their professor in his apartment. They were going to have a study session at his residence but they found him dead. When I got to the scene, they were extremely upset. I called for a supervisor because it was not a natural death (hanging), and they sent Zone Sergeant McGreevy to the scene. By this time, I had gotten all of the young men upstairs into another apartment. When McGreevy arrived, I brought him to the apartment of the deceased and showed him what was going on. I also asked him how long I was going to have to hang around with this guy and he threatened to hit me in the head!

* * *

The next case I had was in the town of Guilderland and it involved a call for assistance in an apartment complex. I responded and no one else was at the scene. A young girl about 19 years of age, lets me into the apartment. She is wearing only a thin bra and panties and she really looks good. She takes me into the bathroom. There is a man in the bathtub completely naked and he appears to be deceased. I check for vitals and there are none. She had gotten back into the tub with the man and was holding him up and all the water was gone out of the tub. I had tried mouth to mouth with negative results and soon the ambulance arrived and took care of the man.

* * *

Another medical case I had in the town of Colonie involved a neighbor calling in because she had not noticed her neighbor in a day or so. I went to the scene and entered the residence and located the old lady on the floor in her bedroom with a broken hip. I contacted the Colonie Police Department as they were in charge of dispatching the ambulance calls and they sent two police cars to the scene. I asked the one officer why they brought two vehicles and he advised that they had one paramedic car and a regular patrol. Their regulations at that time required the paramedic to stay with the injured person so he would have to ride to the hospital in the ambulance in order to remain with the injured person. The other officer would have to follow in his car to bring the first officer back to the scene to get his own car back.

* * *

A friend of mine who was a Sergeant on the Guilderland Department had a similar call for a woman who had not been seen. He went to the residence and located the women at the foot of her cellar stairs. He saw no movement from her and thought she had died. He picked up a phone and called the county coroner, started to describe what was going on and the women sits up and says, "What are you doing in my cellar?" When Doug, the Sergeant recovered enough to speak, the lady told him she always rests on the cellar floor when it is hot out. Now he had to tell the coroner it is all a big mistake and hangs up.

* * *

Another guy named Allen located a missing person on the rear porch floor of her house lying down. He takes his nightstick out and breaks the window. The woman jumps to her feet and says, "Why are you breaking my window?" She was another one who sleeps on the cool floor. Many people might not believe this but there are people who like to rest on the cool floor in the summertime.

Missing Property Located

A new case for me started with a call in Guilderland Center to interview a subject who is a contractor in the old army depot. The guy is from the deep south and wants to report that one of his employees stole a vehicle and a load of tools, some of which were very expensive. He explained that he installed refer units in warehouses and had a contract to build some in Guilderland Center. He gives me the information he has on the man he thinks did it, but it is all messed up and backwards. Even the subjects name is not right. I interviewed some of the other workers and they advise me the suspect likes to hang out at a small bar in Colonie. I go over to the bar and interview the bartender who knows the guy right off the bat. The bartender also says the subject has been talking about going to New York City. I contact Communications at

Loudonville and send a File 1 to the attention of the New York City Police Department. A File 1 is a message reporting a stolen vehicle.

I gave them a full description of the stolen vehicle and when I talked to the bartender he told me the guy traveled by taxi every time he was at the bar. No one remembers the name of the cab company. A few days later the NYPD located the vehicle and towed it to an impound area. I contact the owner and gave him the information. I also advised him that when he brings the car back to my area he is not to disturb the interior as I want to check it first. He agrees and sends a man to get the vehicle. The next day it is back. I searched the interior and located a taxicab card with the driver's name on it and the company involved. I patrolled to the place listed and spoke to the dispatcher, who claims he knows nothing.

I speak to his boss who advises him to assist me and while checking the files I locate calls from the industrial park to the cab company. They were always to the same driver and the drop point is a bar on Central Avenue, (the one I already checked). I return to the bar and the bartender has a small TV that he had forgotten the missing man had given him. The cab driver was a good source of information and I recovered most of the missing tools. The case was turned over to the BCI but no information was recovered as to the missing man's actual name or residence.

An Unfortunate Regular

Another man I dealt with on a regular basis was involved with the town because he had over one hundred thousand vehicle tires on his property. No matter what the town would do, he did not take any action to reduce the pile. He took all of the used tires from any auto shop looking for a place to dump them and they came by the truck full! I believe this was a scheme to make money as he had no income and did not work or want to work.

One of my earlier contacts with him involved a fire at his residence. When the fire Department arrived they found the fire was confined to the second floor. The fire department found that someone started a fire in the bathtub for warmth, which caused the fire. The problem was the bathtub was made of fiberglass and it had not been used in years because the occupants did not wash.

Another thing the occupant used to do was shoot deer out the back window of his residence. The fire department once had been called to pump out the cellar and one of the firemen later told me the occupant was butchering a deer while he was pumping out the cellar. I realized that it was April and it is not open season on

271

deer. I then took a ride to check this deer out. Not to my surprise, the occupant had no permit to have the deer in his kitchen or his living room, which is where he was cutting it up.

While I was at the residence I noticed that every light in the house was on. I checked the meter and found that someone had jumped the meter to get free power. I called the power company for the occupant and they agreed. When they received the warrant, they sent it to me to execute it. I had a power man get the warrant to me in a couple of days and gave the occupant a free ride to the court. I knew he liked getting things free, so why not?

A couple of months prior to this I had a call that someone was standing in the occupant's driveway shooting a pistol at the edge of the road. When I arrived at the scene, the people with the gun were gone but shell casings for a pistol were all over the ground. The occupant said there had been no one there. I was sure the man was lying, but there was not much I could do about it.

He appeared in court for one of his cases I don't know which one, and he had the public defender to represent him. The occupant wants to report six tires have been stolen from his supply of one hundred thousand tires. I ask him how he knows six tires are missing. His lawyer entered the conversation by saying he has them all numbered. The attorney had a shit eating grin on his face as the occupant answers "That's right I had them all numbered." I had been dealing with this public defender for years and I knew he had a sense of humor. I referred to him as the occupant's attorney after this caper.

Armed Robbery

Another armed robbery case I was involved with occurred on route 20 in the town of Guilderland. It occurred at a gas station at night and involved a subject with a rifle. I was one of the first people at the scene and the attendant was a good witness and described the subject very well. He further stated that he did not believe a vehicle was involved as he went outside as soon as the robber left and he never heard a motor start. I contacted Troop Headquarters and requested a K-9 at the scene. My dog Baretta had passed away from a heart condition. They advised me after a pause that Trooper Butterfield and Investigator McKeen were on their way. I waited about thirty minutes and troop contacted me to advise that Mckeen had decided the perpetrator must have had a car, and we should return to patrol.

About a few days later, one of the residents that lived in the rear of the gas station was walking in his yard and found a rifle. When he picked it up it discharged a bullet. No one was hit and the man called the police who recovered the gun. The lab raised the altered serial number on the rifle. By tracing the number they located the owner and the robbery was closed by arrest. This might have occurred if they had approved the dog in the first place and let it track the robber. Then the neighbor would not have fired the rifle by accident, endangering himself and his neighbors.

Sovereign Citizens

Another group of people that I learned to deal with were Sovereign Citizens. They are people that believed they were not required to have insurance on their vehicles or to have them registered or inspected. One of my early contacts with a sovereign citizen was at a State Police road check on Fort Hunter Road in the town of Guilderland. I stopped a pickup truck and instead of pulling over to the side of the road, the man started to drive into the wooded area along side of the road.

He finally stopped when he had to and I approached the vehicle and knocked on the window. He looked at me and then turned his head. I knocked again with my flashlight a little louder and he looked at me. I told him the next knock is coming through the glass and he opened the door window. Everything that could be

274

expired was, and the plates were switched. He also told me I could not tow the truck because it was too far from the road and that he was a Sovereign Citizen and none of the laws applied to him. He told me I could not take any action, as I was not a Police Officer. I advised him he was under arrest and the tow truck was in route to get his truck. Now he suddenly has to go to the bathroom. We are very close to a firehouse and I can see it has a fireman working inside of the building. I start over there with him in tow. He had no cuffs on him yet, as someone is going to handle his weiner and it is not going to be me! I get close enough to the fireman to ask him if my defendant can use his bathroom and he gives me the okay.

This is when the defendant started to ask the fireman to help him as I will not let him call his lawyer and this is an illegal arrest. I told the fireman that I was sorry I let the defendant come into his firehouse. I handcuffed the defendant and brought him out to the troop car to continue to the station. While we were at the firehouse, I let him use the phone and shortly after we arrive at the Guilderland station, someone is at the door. When I answer it, I have another Sovereign subject who must confer with his friend, my defendant. He also explained to me why I had to let him go on his way and started to show me all his copies of the Magna Carta and other laws that would make it very clear to me why I should release him. I continued to do my paperwork then I told the friend to get out and went on with my arrest. I arrested this subject on about five other traffic stops and towed his car each time (towing seemed to bother him so much). The last thing I remember hearing of him was he was involved in a double fatal accident. Two people in the other car were killed. He was operating while revoked, and the car was registered and insured.

Laughing Gas

One of the incidents that occurred with me while I was working happened in Saratoga County. It involved a call for a suspicious person at a residence. I drove to the residence involved and no one was around. I walked over to the garage and looked into the window. I noticed a large canister in the middle of the garage floor and it looked to be covered with a white foam. As I look at it, a man enters the garage from the residence, goes over to the tank and leans on it. Even though I bang on the widows in an attempt to get his attention, he pays no attention to me. He goes back into the house without acknowledging my presence. At this time, I believe the canister has some sort of substance in it that is forming a layer of frost on the container as it escapes from a leak. I enter the garage by opening the overhead door. I try to hold my breath long enough and I turned the valve to the off position and discovered the substance in the container

276

was laughing gas. The man was getting high on the gas. It was the same type used by a dentist. This guy's hands were covered with large blisters from holding the tank while he was using the gas. Sergeant Jim Hughes arrived at the scene and helped me with the case. The subject was transported in an ambulance for medical treatment and later arrested.

Duck Bob!

One of the funniest cases that occurred happened in the East Greenbush area and involved my favorite Lady Trooper, Moe. She was involved with an assist for a BCI arrest of a subject at a residence in that area. They approached the defendant at his residence and knocked on the door. The subject invited them in and the BCI man attempts to arrest the man for a crime. Now a fight starts and the bad guy and the investigator roll down the stairs into the cellar. Now this is the bad guy's house and he knows his way around. The Investigator has never been in this cellar. The bad guy jumps to his feet runs through the cellar and out the door to the driveway.

His car was blocked in by the police car which was running. He jumps in and off he goes in the State Police Vehicle. At the time, I am working the road with Bill Ennis. We are contacted by the dispatcher who assigns us a position at the Massachusetts state border to look for the missing state police vehicle. We are busting a gut especially when the duty captain comes over the troop radio requesting the subject by name to return the vehicle. Later we found out that Moe was trying to assist the Investigator in the struggle and she attempted to strike the bad guy with a large metal flashlight and hit the Investigator instead. For years later Troopers would say to the Investigator, "Duck Bob, Moe will hit you and everything will be alright!" Bob went on to be a colonel in the state police before he retired. They did get the car back and arrested the bad guy.

The Defendant

Another subject I had much contact with as a Trooper started when the kid was about twelve years old. I stopped him walking on a back road. He had a pack of smokes in his shirt pocket and was just walking along. I noticed he was wearing a large set of boots. We had a brief conversation about him smoking and he told me he smoked in front of his parents and in the house. About two days later I received a complaint of a burglary in the same area, I had interviewed this subject. At the location of the burglary, I find the owner very upset because the front door of his residence had been smashed and it was a brand new door that he had not had time to paint yet. The doors were very expensive and they were two that opened from the center.

278

Inside the residence the only sign of a burglary was a half-gallon of Ice cream that had been in the freezer had been removed and set on the table. Some of the ice cream was consumed, but the burglar put it back in the lower section of the refrigerator and it melted all over. Nothing else is stolen or broken in the house and on the damaged door, there are very clear footprints of a large boot. I arrange to visit the kid I had talked to with the large boots on and low and behold the boot prints match. He admits to doing the burglary and I arrest him and turn him over to the BCI as the crime is a felony. It was my first contact with the defendant, but I would have many more encounters.

* * *

On another case, he stole a motorcycle from a man. It was gone for a while and I had not seen him around. One day I was assigned a recruit to ride my shift with me and I went looking for my defendant, as the crime was the type he committed. I knew some older people who lived in a residence on a back road. When I asked them if they had seen my defendant, they said he was in the trailer across the road.

As I entered the trailer, I saw him at the other end with a red motorcycle. The one I was looking for was

279

green, so I walked through the trailer and he smiles as if we are old friends. After I read him his rights I start with, "I am through screwing around with you. Where is that motorcycle?" He knows I am serious and he dropped the smile and says, "It's in your hand." I look down and realize the motorcycle he is working on is the stolen motorcycle only it has a fresh coat of paint. I arrest him. The people that lived in the closest house feel sorry for him even though he is a thief. We returned the machine to its rightful owner and it was a good learning experience for the recruit.

* * *

One of my other contacts with this defendant involved him entering a garage and stealing a motorcycle from a man who treated his machine better than his wife. It was in like-new condition when it was stolen. I must have been off or on vacation because I went after my defendant as soon as I heard of the theft. When I got the machine back, everything that could be broken was. It was actually an all-terrain vehicle and it was almost totally destroyed. I recovered it behind the defendant's residence in the woods and arrested him for it. The damage also caused the vehicle to have to be towed and when the owner got the tow bill, he was wild because of the cost. He wrote a letter asking why the trooper had to call a tow truck that was as big as an aircraft carrier to tow his bike. Most Troopers calling for a tow truck cannot request any special truck unless it is at the owner's request. The dispatcher keeps a list of tow trucks and they are supposed to follow it in order so that one truck is not getting more calls than another.

* * *

At this time the defendant is in his early twenties. As I am working one night I overhear a notice from the Town of Colonie Police Department on the Troop radio that they are looking for my defendant. The name and date of birth are his but they have the height about twelve inches shorter than he is. I contact them on the phone and advise them of the mistake. Shortly after that, they cancel the notice and I take a ride over to the Colonie Police Department. They have my defendant in a holding cell in the basement of the station. He was sitting in a corner of his cell with his head soaking in a five-gallon pail of water trying to get the burn out from the pepper gas that was used to subdue him. I busted on him and told him "I never used gas to subdue you. Why did you go out of town to get arrested?"

* * *

I knew he had moved to Schenectady and I had read some articles in the paper where he had been stabbed. I did not like to drop one of my regulars, but it happens. Before he moved, one of his neighbors felt sorry for him and brought him to my residence while I was having dinner with my family. The man left my defendant in the car and he came up on my porch and knocked on my door. I went out and exchanged greetings. The man told me he had my defendant in the car and told me maybe we could talk things over, I advised him he would have to leave and if the defendant came back on my property, I was going to arrest him for trespass. The man left with the defendant and I later ran into him some place in town. He told me after he took the defendant for the ride to my house, the defendant stole something from him and he hoped he never saw him again.

* * *

Another thing the defendant was starting to do as he grew older, which was odd, was he started to hang around with children that were a lot younger then he was. At least once, he was carrying a firearm while in the presence of these kids. I went to his house and interviewed the father of the defendant and he agreed with me that his kid should not be around any firearms without supervision. After that, I had no information on him being involved with a gun. His last involvement with me was a stolen motorcycle that I recovered at his neighbor's house across the street from where he lived.

282

Trooper Tommy Jensen, (Tommy Perfect), located it for me buried under a brush pile.

Working at the Academy

When the State Police Academy first opened, I was assigned as an instructor for a total of seven weeks. It took me off the road and I did not care for it. One of the things that we had to do was lock our firearms in a room in the basement and pick them up when it was time to leave. The academy person in charge of the key was never on time. Another thing they had done was assign each trooper a bedroom. I knew this because someone sat on the bed I was issued and never used. This caused me to get a note from the academy staff for not making my bed. When I responded to the note and explained that I only lived twelve miles from the academy and I would not be using the bed, I was informed to stop by each day and make sure it was made.

While in route to my residence from the academy, (we were allowed to use the state's vehicle to go home in) I had picked up my revolver and put it in the holster without loading it. As I am going east of state highway 5 in the town of Colonie, I notice a vehicle that looks like it should be checked. I contact the dispatcher and file check the vehicle and bigger then shit it comes back a file 1 (stolen car) out of a Midwestern state. As soon as they

283

give me this information, they are calling me to make sure I am all right and to get my exact location. I still am going east but I am trying to steer the troop car with my knees so I can load my revolver. The caper turns out to be a file 1 that the home department failed to cancel so I got it cancelled and we all went on our way. That was one division regulation I was more careful with after that experience.

Keough and Rector

On another patrol with Scotty Rector just coming out of the Guilderland station we entered State Route 20, going in a westerly direction. In the middle of the road are two people about to do battle. One is armed with a length of chain and the other has a baseball bat. When I get close enough to them on foot, I yell, "DROP IT!" I heard the chain hit the pavement quickly but the guy holding the bat looks me right in the eye. He keeps holding the bat and turns toward his opponent. I gave the subject a little tap with the flashlight, the bat hit the road and made quite a lot of noise. The man then listened very well and the event was over (I do not remember what they were fighting over) and we resumed patrol.

* * *

On another night with Rector we came upon a man parked in the middle of the highway and when we approached the operator he was very drunk. He did not want to get out of his car. I reached in and got ahold of him and his leg came off in my hand. I had no idea how to reattach it, so he was destined to hop until we got him where he was going. We arrested him, administered the test and eventually sent him on his way.

We ended up in court in the city of Albany with a lady District Attorney. The man brought a woman to court with him and she testified that she had been the operator of the vehicle, but had left the scene on foot before we arrested him. The Assistant District Attorney did her best to attempt to get the truth out of her with negative results. When we returned to the assistant District Attorney's office, her father would have been upset at the language she used to describe the female witness but I would have to agree with the ADA.

Cherry Picker on Fire

On one occasion when I pulled out of State Police Loudonville Troop G Headquarters to start my shift, I noticed the traffic light on route 9 was out of service. I thought someone might have hit a pole. As I was going north I checked each one. As I got to the area of Hoffman's Playground, I saw a large truck equipped with a cherry picker (a bucket able to let a man go high above the vehicle and work on wires). The bucket was raised up but there was no man in it and the bar that lifts it was resting against the power lines. The power lines had left a burn mark on the bar. In the general area of the truck three men are standing around looking up at the bucket and talking. I also noticed that there was a piece of rope with a wooden block on the end that they had thrown over the wire in an attempt to pull the wire away from the truck. One of the men tells me he is going to move the truck away from the wire and I tell him he cannot do that. I wanted to wait for the power company personnel. I had already called them and they said it would only take a minute. I tell him if you touch the truck, I will arrest you!

At this time, the power company arrives and the foreman comes over to me with fire in his eyes wanting to know if I threw the rope over the wire. I let him know I had nothing to do with that and that it was that way when I arrived. At this time all the tires on the truck burst into flames and are burning quite well. There is a slight mist in the air from a rainstorm, and the power company guy is not so mad any more. They shut off the power, moved the truck away and we all went on our way. I have no idea why he would blame me for the rope on the wire? Could it be he did not like Troopers?

Keough and Ellis

Another man I worked nights with was Walt Ellis. I always thought we got along fairly well and Walt was a wiz at the manual for the State Police. He passed the Sergeant test and went on to become the station commander at the Governor's Detail. We had one caper that occurred in the town of Guilderland on the midnight shift. We had a call about a suspicious vehicle parked in a wooded area in Guilderland and we started to the scene. As we arrived, we locate the vehicle and it is stuck in the mud. It is not the type of vehicle that should even be in the mud. As we are looking the scene over, we get a second call from our dispatcher that they had a call from a tow truck operator who has the owner with him and is on his way to get the car.

We acknowledged the call and within two minutes, the dispatcher is back on the air telling us that he file checked the vehicle on his own and it came back a stolen car out of Pennsylvania (good dispatcher). Walt and I decided to ambush the people coming in to recover the stolen car but we have to hurry. Walt goes up the road to get behind them and I remain with the stolen car. In a very short time, I hear the tow truck coming through the woods and when it gets close I stop it, gun in hand. Two men are in the tow truck.

I put both subjects on the ground and the one man drops a large bowie knife on the ground before he gets down. I can now hear Walt yelling, "Stop Police!" The chase in on with a third subject. He soon runs the bad guy down and we identify the driver and leave with a good arrest. The defendant that Walt chased down had a large pistol holster on his belt. No gun, but he had the holster.

State Police Bloopers

At one time, in town of Colonie, the State Police had a patrol in that town and it was very active. As the town hired more officers the State Police patrols were sent elsewhere. One of the spots the patrols would meet was in the area of the Latham traffic circle. It was easy to spot the drunks because they would always have trouble making it around the circle without hitting the rail or curb. Once they hit something, there was the cause for a stop, if not an arrest. I can remember one night a State Police patrol was sitting at the parking lot, and a Colonie unit pulled in beside him. They are shooting the breeze for five minutes when a drunk enters the circle. He runs into the guide rail and takes off. The trooper gets all excited hits the gas and runs into the Colonie unit parked beside him because his wheel was turned and he did not know it. Both of the units have to call for a supervisor to police the accident and the drunk got away.

In that same area there was a bar. A vehicle in the roadway was struck by another car which knocked the front seat out of the car and all the occupants. The vehicle was still in gear and running. A trooper arrives at the scene, gets out of the police car and looks the scene over for a few minutes. He then runs and jumps into the moving car hurting his backside on the exposed metal in the vehicle, but he gets it stopped. The people from the bar actually cheer for him when he stopped the car.

Keough and Khachadourian

At one time Guilderland had a large church made mostly of wood standing on Route 146 in Guilderland Center. One night, the building caught fire and although the firemen fought the flames as hard as they could the church burned fiercely. At the scene of the fire Trooper William Khachadourian (AKA Khach) was conducting an investigation in regards to the cause of the fire. He found a fuel station attendant and he interviewed him. He admitted to selling some dry gas to a young man just before the fire. Khach located the man and after a brief interview, the subject admitted to starting the fire at the church. He was arrested and convicted of the fire that burned for two days and totally destroyed the church. I do not remember the sentence he got for the crime but a more suitable punishment would have been to turn him over to the firemen who fought the blaze, smelled the smoke and broke their backs trying to put out the fire. The church has been rebuilt and it is a wonderful looking building made mostly of stone at the same location the other church had stood for a very long time.

Keough and Ditton

One other trooper I do not believe I have yet mentioned that also worked in the Guilderland station was Robert Ditton. Bob and I had some good cases together. One that comes to my mind is Bob is riding alone on Becker road in the town of Guilderland. He comes up behind a van truck that becomes very erratic. As he gets closer, he turns on his red lights and the van pulls over. Bob dismounted and approached the vehicle and he hears a loud gunshot. He draws his own revolver and orders the operator out of the vehicle. As the man steps out, a large cloud of smoke exits the vehicle. There are three other men trying to shoot deer from the edge of the road illegally and they believe it is quicker to have your gun loaded (although the possession of a loaded gun in a vehicle is illegal).

When they spotted the Trooper's car, they attempted to unload the gun and it discharged. The shotgun slug went through the rear doors of the van, struck the front of the troop car and ended up alongside of the front tire of the Trooper's vehicle. Bob arrested the violators and took the gun into custody. If I had been with him, I am sure I would have had to change my pants.

On another patrol when Bob Ditton and I were working together, we had stopped a vehicle and the operator ran from the scene. Bob ran him down and we arrested him. While Bob was taking care of his first capture, the other occupant in the vehicle exits the car and runs like hell across the highway. I start after him and he comes to a fence about fifteen feet high. He started to climb it. By the time I got to the fence he was already on top of it. I saw a gate and it opened. I went through and he hit the ground right in front of me.

I jumped right on top of him and placed an arm bar on him. When I interviewed him as to why he ran, he was full of answers. As it turned out he thought he was wanted but there was no warrant in the computer for him and we even checked by phone with his hometown Police with negative results. We had to throw him back... that fish was out of season.

Billy

At one time, we had a recruit in Guilderland by the name of Joe Ficarella. On a night when Joe and I were in the same car, we stopped in to visit the Guilderland town court that was in session. Many of the people were lined up in a hallway waiting to see town judge. I spot the clerk of the court walking toward me and she is crying. She takes my arm and walks away from the court pulling me along. She whispers, "Billy is here and he has a hammer." I look down the row of people and I spot Billy large as can be and he has a carpenter's hammer in his hand waiting to see the judge. The man is crazy and she knows it because he is always getting arrested for minor things and spends a lot of time in court.

The man is about six-foot-tall and solid muscle. He has no car and almost all of his travel is done by bike. That is where all the muscle comes from. I change my direction of travel and brief Joe as quick as I can. I slide onto the bench next to Billy grabbing the hammer with my right hand. Billy says, "That's my hammer! Let it go!" The whole time I was trying to calm Billy down but then he starts to cry and demands I release his hammer. I ask him how he got the hammer and why he brought it to court and he answers. I try to explain that I have to keep the hammer until his court appearance is over. I tell him to look around no one else has a hammer. He lets go of it and I promise to return it.

On one of my other contacts with Billy he was wearing new boots and I had a case with a peeping Tom who was spotted in an area next to his residence. I spotted Billy in Dunkin Doughnuts and stopped to chat with him. I asked Bill to show me the bottom of his boots and I realized the pattern was not like the one I was looking for so I said goodnight and left. Later that night an unknown person contacted the Selkirk station by phone and told the desk person that he was going to stomp Trooper Keough to death with his new boots. This was just his way of saying hello.

At one time, the Guilderland P.D. attempted to arrest him at his residence and they had a hard time fighting with him to get him out of his apartment. He was just a very strong person. When they got him out, his apartment was as neat as a pin and everything was as clean as it could be. After the altercation the front door was bent.

Dynamite and Fuel

On one occasion, the station contacted me by radio and told me to go to exit 14 off interstate 87 and assist with an accident investigation. The call was strange because it was out of my area and in a different zone. At the time I got the call, I was going southbound. I then pulled into a U-turn and went north but as soon as I got the car turned around, I saw a large column of dark smoke going up in the sky. Troop Headquarters advised me that a truck hauling fuel oil had run into the rear of another truck hauling dynamite about 20 miles north of my location and the rig was on fire. That explained the column of smoke I could see from 20 miles away. By the time I got to the scene, the dynamite driver had used his head and just kept going until he cleared the fire so his rig was clear and the fire department had beat down the remaining fuel fire. That forty thousand pounds of explosives would make a very large explosion under the right circumstances but because the drivers were on the ball everything was all right.

Conclusion

I had always handled 95 percent of the dog calls, especially the night calls. My dog had a very impressive record and did very good work. He was part of our family. The dog and I worked until 1982. I went to be a Master of Ceremonies at a promotion party one night. That night my son took, Baretta out for walk and the dog had a heart attack and died. That was the end of my dog handling for the State Police. My kids were so upset I felt I had to get them another dog. They named the new German Shepard I got them Baretta also. They enjoyed his company until he died about five years later of cancer.

Working as a Trooper was always good and I enjoyed it very much. On the night patrol, the average person could not understand the sort problems that may occur between two men. For example, one may have gas, and the other unfortunate person is forced to inhale his stink. One has to burp all night long and stink the car up with that! One guy wears long underwear and likes the heat on low. The other wears no underwear, wants the heat on high and complains if the temperature gets below 72 degrees. I was able to adjust to my partners pretty well and I think most of the men I worked with got along with me fairly well.

In 1998, I reached the maximum age of fifty-seven

and I had to retire. I ended up with thirty-five years because I had credit for one year in the marines during the Vietnamese War and one year of service on the Capitol Police. I enjoyed the people I worked with. I honestly think I worked with some of the best men and women on the job. Many of the young men I worked with went on to be officers in the State Police.

Made in the USA
Columbia, SC
25 September 2017